Parent Fatigue Syndrome:

What To Do When Conventional Wisdom Is Not Very Wise

For our children,

Joanna & Blethyn

Joanna Hulton, Ph.D.

with Blethyn Hulton

St
Owl

Huntington, New York

Parent Fatigue Syndrome:
What To Do When Conventional Wisdom Is Not Very Wise

Book cover by
Laura Varrone

Published by
Studio Owls Inc.
Huntington, New York

Library of Congress Control Number: 201394790
ISBN: 978-0-9898417-2-6

Publisher's Cataloging-in-Publication data

Hulton, Joanna.
    Parent fatigue syndrome : what to do when conventional wisdom is not very wise / by Joanna Hulton, Ph.D. , with Blethyn Hulton.
    p. cm.
    ISBN 978-0-9898417-2-6
    Includes bibliographical references and index.

1. Parenting. 2. Parenting -- Psychological aspects. 3. Parents. 4. Child rearing. 5. Parent and child. 6. Communication in the family. 7. Child development. I. Hulton, Blethyn. II. Title.

HQ755.8 .H85 2013
649.1/222 --dc23   201394790

Printed in the United States of America

For all comments and inquires, email:
editor@parentfatiguesyndrome.com

For
Corey Alexandra Lein

Contents

Author's Note

All the vignettes in this book are inspired by the families with whom I have worked over the years. To protect their privacy I have changed names, places, and other identifying details. While each story is a composite of different families, the treatment issues and interventions realistically represent my clinical experiences. Any similarity to individuals and situations that you may know is purely coincidental.

Introduction

It was my last appointment of the day. I was in session with a young father who had been working for months trying to understand his kids so that he could speak "childrenese" more fluently. On this particular evening, we were talking about the difficulty of being a parent in today's world. Together we understood that the way he had been parented was not only unhelpful but also causing painful conflicts; chronic dissatisfaction had left him feeling depleted and unhappy.

At one point he leaned back against the sofa and sighed, "Do you know what I am suffering from? Parent Fatigue Syndrome." With that phrase, he captured what so many of the parents who come to my office are experiencing.

I am writing this book to share with you what I have learned about children's emotional growth and development. This knowledge comes from thirty years of both professional and personal experience working with children, parents, and educators as a mother, teacher, and psychotherapist.

I intend this book to give you a better understanding of yourself and your children and to strengthen your confidence in your ability to explore the available information so that you can combat Parent Fatigue Syndrome in your own way.

How did we get here, and why has it become so exhausting to raise children?

There is considerable research explaining how individuals re-identify with their own parents after having children of their own. We are all hardwired to scan our memories so that we can engage in the tremendous task of being a parent. It is during these times that we often collide with the conventional wisdom of the past.

Some of the "wisdom" sounds like this:

Do what I say, not what I do!

Spare the rod, spoil the child!

Children are to be seen and not heard!

Speak only when spoken to!

Only girls do that!

Only boys do that!

Respect your elders!

Wait until your father gets home!

And how about these, which I gathered from a book of vintage quotations:

"Tired mothers find that spanking takes less time than reasoning, and penetrates sooner to the seat of memory."

"Who loves well chastises well."

"My mother protects me from the world, my father threatens me with it."

Alas, some of the wisdom passed down to us clearly has no place in our post-modern age, where our children have both greater freedoms and fewer responsibilities. Children of the present learn early on that they have some of the same entitlements of self-expression and self-determination as adults. At the same time, children do not play the same economic role today, with its responsibilities, that they did a century ago. During the pre-industrial era, children may have farmed the land and tended the livestock; at the very least, each of them was required to make a contribution to the survival of the family. It is probable that very few of *our* children work the family farm in the morning. Quoting Penelope Leach in *Children First*, "Children in the post-industrial west have the longest compulsory childhood that the world has ever seen. With all those years of enforced dependence ahead of them, we have to learn that letting them take their own time over growing up is what is best for them now, and what will best help them fulfill their own potential when they are grown. It will not be an easy lesson."

As parents we are in conflict. We need to believe that the values of the past are helpful since not being or acting like our parents might confirm our worst fear, that we as children at times were not treated well. And so we cling to the conventional wisdom of the past while we are trying to move our children successfully into the future.

Alternately, we may have promised ourselves that we would never do to our children what our parents did to us; but from this impossible promise we can end up hating the very child that causes us to behave like the parent we vowed never to become.

Such conflicts create enormous fatigue. But what is a parent to do? We can start by revisiting that important question: What is the purpose of children, and how do they contribute to today's family?

Some sociologists over the years have suggested that we have become fascinated with being part of a leisure class and take pride in having economic surplus. While this might describe a better life for all of us, it may also adversely influence how we encourage our children to spend their time; the "longest compulsory childhood" has pressured us to find ways to fill their time productively. In 2010, in light of our recent economic downturn, one must additionally wonder how and if this further complicates how we feel about our so-called prosperity.

We want our children to be smart, capable, and successful; and we worry that they will not be ready for the competitive world that awaits. As a result, we have created some of our own conventional wisdom. It sounds like this:

Earlier to school, the smarter and more social the child.

Start training early, or they will fall behind.

Deprive the medication, set your child up for failure.

Some results of this "wisdom" are in. In his book *Generation Rx*, Greg Critser sites example after example of young adults who depended on drugs to learn yet felt crippled when faced with the important challenges of college and beyond. For his part, David Elkind, in his classic book *The Hurried Child*, warns us about the dangers of growing up too quickly. His eloquence brings into clear relief the preciousness of each stage of a child's development. He challenges us to not be seduced by a society that pushes children forward without understanding their essential needs.

But what do children really need, and how do we as parents provide for them?

Over the years I have read many articles and books about parenting and child development. While each of them impressed and informed me, I did not always feel supported and understood. Many times, differing opinions confused me as I tried to cobble together a unified approach that would help me feel confident and comfortable. In addition, these books contradicted what I had learned from my parents, only perpetuating my low sense of self-efficacy. What could I do if indeed I was to choose a new path?

I believe that our evolutionary purpose is to keep the tradition of one's family while innovating so as to adapt to the ever-changing world. In doing so, we honor our parents, have empathy for their life-journey, and most importantly give ourselves permission to create a caregiving style that they might not fully agree with or understand.

This book will show how a lack of understanding between you and your own parents over child-rearing can leave you feeling fatigued. However, by allowing yourself to parent more freely but no less conscientiously, with the tools and information I provide, you will feel the enthusiasm associated with successful parenting.

The book will impart child-development information in a way that enhances rather than inhibits each parent's creation of their own parenting style so that you can be inspired in the same way that an artist is inspired to use his paints and imagination to express his unique understanding of the world.

I encourage you to use your canvas in a way that best suits you and your family. I expect that at times you will be moved by the book; at times you may be moved to stop reading it. But hopefully you will keep reading. And offsetting the awkwardness you feel at some points, at others you will smile, maybe even laugh, as you read the stories I tell, all collected from the wonderful families that I have had the privilege to work with over the years.

I hope that you will finally feel understood and in the company of other well-meaning parents. You are *not* alone; like many others you are are doing your best to prepare your children for the world that awaits them.

I intend for you to use this book as a point of departure, an inspiration for personal creativity. At the end of each chapter, I will offer additional readings so that you can further your individual interest and growth.

There is really no one way to parent. The beauty will be in what each of you does with the knowledge you gain.

Let us begin.

Part One

Ghosts of Parents Past

In every nursery there are ghosts. They are the visitors from the unremembered past of the parents: the uninvited guests at the christening. Under favorable circumstances the unfriendly and unbidden spirits are banished from the nursery and return to their subterranean dwelling place ... This is not to say that ghosts cannot invent mischief from their burial places. Even among families where the love bonds are stable and strong, the intruders from the parental past may break through the magic circle in an unguarded moment, and a parent and his child might find themselves reenacting a moment or scene from another time with another set of characters.

— Selma Fraiberg

As we begin to decide how we want to be as parents, we inevitably recall our own parents or caregivers and re-identify with them. This "mental work," which follows naturally from our daily acts of caregiving, becomes an intense and highly influential "remembering context" of our experiences and feelings when we were children. While we as parents can be sure that this remembering will happen, it is not assured that the process will happen consciously, through stories we share with chosen witnesses, or unconsciously, through episodes with our children that are "reenacting a moment or scene from another time with another set of characters." This difference is crucial. Whether our remembering occurs consciously or unconsciously determines whether we will be able to liberate ourselves from the ghosts in the nursery or become dragged down by them and engulfed in parent fatigue.

If pursued consciously, the act of remembering is a gift that you give yourself and your child for it is only after we speak about and understand the past that we can use the memories to move freely into the future. Only by doing our best to recall both our good and bad childhood experiences can we redefine ourselves, and so establish the proper priorities of claims upon our time and emotions to meet the all-consuming needs of children.

The gift of remembering may not come easily. As we consciously recall our past as children, we will likely come face to face with our ambivalence towards our parents. With one patient of mine, a young father, it was only after some exhausting digging into his childhood that we could begin to understand how parenting had become such a chore.

David remembered his father as a smart but frustrated man who bullied his wife and family, a rage-aholic version of the 1950s TV show "Father Knows Best." David's father was a blue-collar worker with a high-school education who articulated a sharp though always oppressively cynical understanding of local and national politics. The episodes of frustrated rage often accompanied the father's do-it-yourself efforts, such as repairs to the family car. At such times, David, the middle child, stood between his father and his siblings. As the father realized that the repairs were beyond his ability, the explosion of anger would send everyone into hiding; but David would lovingly stay behind, running back to forth to the garage to fetch parts and tools, hoping that his devotion would calm his father down. Instead, his rage would boil to a point that was even too much for David. At the end of this common scene, David's father would be alone in the driveway, kicking and screaming at the car he was trying to mend.

Needless to say, the devoted son received neither any apology from his father nor acknowledgment of the sacrifices he had made; and so he suffered doubly. Not only did he fail in the impossible and undeserved task of helping his father with his anger, he was denied his right as a child to a loving parent who would support him in periods of his own anger and fear.

Grownup and married, David became a father of two. As he guided his children through the storms of their emotions, the memories of his own deprivations as a child distorted his instinctive reactions to his wife and children. This imaginative and sensitive father worked hard to be everything his father was not: lovingly patient, available to his children, and most importantly fixer of all things. As his family grew, the inevitable developmental conflicts began to create a constant source of pressure; but his belief that these conflicts were a result of his inadequacy made it difficult for him to understand that conflict in childhood development is essential for growth. Instead he took each developmental crisis personally, sure that he was the cause.

When trying to discipline the children, he would lose himself in space and time as these experiences became a "remembering context," bringing back the terrifying rage of his father and his helplessness to do anything about it. In such moments, it was all David could do but to remove himself from the room; and afterward, he would apologize endlessly for his misbehavior. It is no surprise that eventually his efforts to perform the important parental task of discipline were ineffective with the children, brought conflicts with his wife, and left him ashamed and drained.

As David shared stories from his childhood with me, I took the role of a caring witness to his childhood trauma. At first his stories were just factual reports; but later on, he was able to express the affect, or feelings, attached to these memories, especially his conflicting fear of and anger toward his beloved father.

In time, David shared his recollections with his wife, which served to cement in the work he did in therapy. In this way, she became another caring witness to his childhood struggles. As a team, they could work together to remain aware of how his traumatic past might invite the ghosts back in.

For some parents, the act of remembering both the facts and the feelings attached to their childhood experiences is too scary; and so they stay buried. But these ghosts wreak havoc nonetheless. The inability to express the feelings associated with childhood memories is what bedeviled my patient Anna.

In our first session, Anna reported that her daughter was exhibiting signs of depression, was unmotivated to go to school, and was no longer interested in trying anything new. At the same time, Anna told me that her daughter, who was clearly very bright, was excelling in all her classes and was enjoying her many after-school activities, where she could display her diverse talents. And while the teachers and after-school instructors heaped praise on the child, Anna down-played her daughter's achievements. It seemed that each compliment caused Anna to worry more and more about her daughter's imperfections. To fight the anxiety, Anna made sure that each hour of her daughter's schedule was accounted for; and as mother and child meticulously honored schedules, it eventually became impossible for Anna, herself a busy profes-sional, to do anything but work and find time for her daugh-ter's activities and homework. Understandably, the mother was an emotional wreck, exhausted and worried by her daughter's very existence. Meanwhile the daughter, naturally needing her mother's approval, could do nothing but continue to achieve; yet with each triumph, she met only her mother's criticism and fatigue. As the reader might expect, eventually the daughter began to fall apart during any activities that tested her abilities. She could not control her emotions and was continually embar-rassing herself and her self-conscious mother in public.

From the outset of our work, Anna was aware of her confusion and anger towards the child she was raising as a single mom. Her anger scared her; and with her extraordinary intellectual curiosity, she began to question me to get a better understanding of that fear. When I suggested that sometimes the experiences we have with our children help us remember our own childhood, she was initially responsive. Over many sessions, she shared the facts of her life story; but I sensed that the attached affect was missing. Anna, also a talented child, had been terribly abused by a jealous older sibling; and a lack of parental attention allowed this abuse to continue for many years. Talented and sensitive, Anna was easily made to feel inferior and helpless by her brother after even the smallest mistake; but Anna had no one else to look up to in order to satisfy her natural need for approval from a comforting adult.

As we worked together to bring her childhood experiences to light, I began to wonder out loud about how she might have felt during these times. I gently suggested to her that some people would think that as a child she must have felt fear and anger on occasion. Her reaction was immediate. Utterly dismayed by my suggestion, she said that she did not remember any such feelings; she was angry that I thought her upbringing could have been abusive; and she wondered how many therapists like me made up tales of abuse that never happened. I realized from her response that the feelings attached to these childhood memories were terrifying. She took my probing as a betrayal, and expressed her disappointment that I, her once trusted guide, was now leading her into uncharted territory, that the person of the therapist whom she unconsciously counted upon to understand the abuse was now the abuser, "forcing her" into conversations that caused pain, anger and fear.

Our work continued; but only when she understood that the perfectionism that she directed at her daughter was a way to repeat the persecution she suffered as a child, could she stop inflicting the unremembered pain onto her own child.

Psychologists sometimes define what Anna was doing to her daughter as "identifying with the aggressor." This is an unconscious process that can occur when a parent with little access to memories of childhood pain takes on the fearsome traits of a previous abuser. In this way the individual is no longer the helpless child but instead the one finally in control. Anna will need to continually check in with her childhood memories as she raises her daughter so that her child's stages of development do not trigger memories that have been long buried, providing yet again a "remembering context" that will impair their relationship.

We can see that the conventional wisdom in the expression "let sleeping dogs lie" can perpetuate unhappiness and cruelty. Rather, a parent needs to remember and reflect upon their own upbringing to prevent the harm of being "bitten in the night."

You may be wondering about your own "ghosts in the nursery." One way to bring these ghosts out into the open is by taking stock of the challenges you are facing with your children. Some of the problems that are keeping you up at night and never seem to get any better may be caused by a lack of information about developmental psychology. In these cases, I hope that the following chapters will provide a friendly and well-informed guide that you can use at a comfortable pace. For other issues, you may need to go deeper to understand how these problems may set the stage for playing out old life-scripts with a new set of actors. I believe that if you can consciously recall these experiences and share them with a caring witness, you can step outside yourself into the light of personal awareness so as to better understand your children and overcome your parent fatigue.

More books to read!

Liberated Parents, Liberated Children: Your Guide To A Happier Family, by Adele Faber and Elaine Mazlish.

Giving The Love That Heals: A Guide For Parents, by Harville Hendrix and Helen Hunt.

The Truth Will Set You Free: Overcoming Emotional Blindness and Finding Your True Adult Self, by Alice Miller.

Intimate Worlds: Life Inside the Family, by Maggie Scarf.

Part Two

*The Absolutely
Essential Needs of Children*

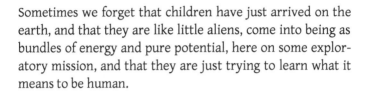

Sometimes we forget that children have just arrived on the earth, and that they are like little aliens, come into being as bundles of energy and pure potential, here on some exploratory mission, and that they are just trying to learn what it means to be human.

— *Martian Child*, 1998

The Need to Be Understood

Being human. It is not so easy especially when one feels misunderstood. Children wake up each morning ready to take on the essential task of early childhood: to be known. It sounds simple, but alas many things prevent it from happening genuinely. As a result, many of us grow into adulthood with inauthentic selves. We may not appear as "aliens," or inauthentic to others; but we are not true to ourselves.

How is it that so many of us lose ourselves while growing up? An adult patient once declared, "I need you to understand me so that I will know who I am." Understanding ourselves comes from feeling understood as children, but being understood can be quite difficult if one's parents are not fluent in "childrenese" or if they are overwhelmed with their own parenting agenda.

For parents "the days are long, the years are short," as one mother put it. Parents themselves are challenged each day as they prepare their children for school and beyond. Every day brings new tasks and conflicts that require us to dig deep, what one parent described as the continual opportunity to "kick open the doors to the primordial stuff of my own childhood."

In the previous chapter I describe how everyday experiences in your early childhood create the template that you use daily to solve the challenges of parenting. Most of these experiences lie waiting for reactivation in your unconscious. "The unconscious mind," as David Brooks describes it in *The Social Animal*, "is most of the mind - not a dark, vestigial place but a creative and enchanted one, where most of the brain's work gets done. . . the realm where character is formed and where our most important life decisions are made." Over time you will discover that the daily interactions with and efforts to understand your children will influence you both consciously and unconsciously, uniquely enabling you to become more self-aware. And the ultimate achievement of this greater self awareness is the opportunity for you to know your most authentic self.

Making Sense Out of Happy, Sad, Angry and Afraid

A prerequisite to authentic humanity is the full expression of the four basic emotions. Much of our current culture readily supports only one emotion, being happy. Children are rarely told that "happiness" is something they should not feel. Instead, this emotion or feeling state is usually accepted, many times allowing parents the opportunity to feel competent and happy themselves. There can be an exception to this rule, which is that a child's expression of happiness is not supported if it leads to over-excitement or unbridled expansiveness, which I will address in the discussion of grandiosity.

But it is when children bump into experiences that induce sadness, anger and fear that parents resort to responses that can inhibit authenticity. How many times have we heard or said, "Don't be scared, there is nothing to be afraid of," or "You are angry over that? I'll give you something to be angry at!" and "Why are you so sad, will this make you feel better?"

Take some time to reflect on your past. What are your earliest memories concerning the four human emotions of happy, sad, angry and afraid? There is a good chance that you were not encouraged to express all your feeling-states as you were growing up. The conventional wisdom "children are to be seen and not heard" was widely accepted; and it prevented many of our own parents from making full sense of their feelings and of our feelings as children. The parenting wisdom passed down to us by our well-meaning parents may be causing conflicts between our child and us: On the one hand we want our children to express themselves, on the other we may worry that they are too precocious and disrespectful.

Suppressing and Repressing Feelings

The parents of six-year-old Sarah started family therapy because they could no longer put up with her "meltdowns." In their minds, she had become so willful and stubborn that they dreaded the end of the school day and the start of the weekend. Even the simple task of Sarah putting on her socks caused stress and conflict; she alternately thought of them as "too scratchy," "too big," "too small" - generally unacceptable.

It was getting harder and harder to get any cooperation from this bright and able child. The more her parents told her to "act her age," the more she would either dissolve into tears or burst into anger.

By contrast, Sarah did very well in school, her academic life providing her with opportunities to feel proud and accomplished. Her teacher mirrored this, describing her as a "perfect young student."

But she was failing socially. She was unable to connect with any of the other kids in the class. To her mother's dismay, she reported daily that the other children did not want to play with her. She felt picked on by the others and indeed was rarely invited to after-school playdates. Often, she would complain of a headache or stomach ache, so she could not play with others; at other times she would sit alone reading or drawing in her art journal. Between her social isolation and domestic outbursts, Sarah's parents were at a loss.

I invited this young family to a play-session, a technique I use to learn how family members interact. Filial play therapy is a wonderful parenting tool I will discuss in greater detail in *Kitchen-Table Therapy*.

During our initial session Sarah decided to use the dollhouse as her family forum. As she picked the objects to place inside the rooms, Mom would intervene with friendly advice on what to pick. As Sarah continued to create scenes in each room, both parents would comment on her choices in a judgmental way. While each of them was trying to encourage a rich experience for Sarah, they were unknowingly squelching her attempt to create her own "story," where she could begin to express her feelings.

After I delicately conveyed this impression to the parents, they began to just watch and listen as Sarah decorated each room with characters of her own making. Although she used all my human toy-figures to represent family members, she chose the "family dog and cat" to express the initial conflict.

We watched Sarah's characters engage in their disagreement. She was relaxed as she proceeded to tell us why the cat and dog were fighting, and we did not interrupt.

After a while the dog and cat went outside the dollhouse, and the tensions rose between the two "human" figures. The play continued to take place in the tiny kitchen. Sarah giggled as she assigned roles to the plastic father and child figures, but her face changed quickly when the plastic father figure stormed out of the kitchen and then back in.

Under Sarah's guiding hand, the child figure then stormed in and out of the kitchen while the plastic father sat still at the table. Following this, the child figure went into the garage, sat in the car, and drove back into the kitchen; but the father figure did not respond. We did not interrupt.

Finally, the dollhouse father and child began to argue hotly at the kitchen table. Sarah then walked both the parent and child figures through the house, each room inviting new recriminations.

At this point Sarah stopped the play action and looked over at her mom and dad sitting quietly on the floor next to her. Her facial expression closed as she spoke for the plastic child figure, "I hate you." We didn't interrupt, but I noticed Sarah's dad stiffening and Mom sighing softly. And Sarah looked worried. I stayed close to her experience by commenting on the changes. She replied, "I don't want to play anymore," and then went quiet.

Feeling that Sarah had expressed enough, I set her up with another activity and invited the parents into my office to talk privately.

I shared my thoughts and observations with the parents and wondered aloud about the noticeable changes in the family's experience, including the dad's body language and the mom's sad exhale in response to their daughter's expression of hating. The mother quickly interjected that Sarah had broken one of her father's most important rules: Never say "I hate you." She explained that it had become an issue at home and had been causing much conflict of late. She revealed that she didn't really understand why he felt so strongly about this; to her they were just words.

I looked over at the father, who was anxious to speak, and asked him what he thought about what his wife had just said. He answered with a long and passionate speech about how disrespectful his child was at times. He expressed his discontent at "being spoken to in that way," and disagreed that "they were just words." And then came the declaration, "I would have never spoken to my parents that way."

Had he ever spoken so disrespectfully as a child, he would have "gotten a good smack in all the right places." His usage of the words "good" and "right" helped me understand the genesis of his parenting style. Here was a father trying his best to have an effective influence on his daughter. His censorship of the word "hate" was what he remembered from his childhood. It worked to keep him in line; and he couldn't understand why it was causing such conflict in his home.

The conversation we started that afternoon became a prominent theme in subsequent sessions. For her part, Sarah's mom remembered a more "democratic environment "growing up, where children were encouraged to voice their opinions. But the father recalled a "do what I say, not what I do" environment where children were quiet and obedient. Keeping one's feelings to oneself was an easy way to stay out of trouble, but not a good way for him to learn to make sense of those feelings. Now, as a parent, Sarah's father could not help his daughter make sense of her feelings because he had not learned to tolerate his own. The lack of support in his emotional life while growing up was now causing conflict that he felt should be smoothed over and silenced rather than understood and contained. When she was unhappy, he would distract her and make her laugh with playful teasing. He quelled her fears by removing her from any situation that could cause discomfort, and over time he let her know that any aggression or anger expressed towards the parents would result in the temporary loss of her favorite toys.

Making matters worse for Sarah, her mother would openly challenge her husband's responses. In his defensive reaction, he would bear down harder and harder, forcing his young child to accommodate herself to his insecurities. Sarah was getting some very strong messages about feelings. On the rare occasion when their expression broke through, they brought conflict between her parents at a time when she needed them most to be in harmony with each other.

I could easily see why this child enjoyed her academic life; it was an intellectual forum where she could use her skills with minimal need to engage in interpersonal relationships. Such relationships and their social interaction required a comfortable, free exchange of feelings for which Sarah had no preparation.

I Before We

Sarah's struggle in her attempt to become an "I" was being thwarted by the denial of her feelings and the resulting unacknowledged unhappiness. As it is for many children, the expression of true feelings — happy, sad, angry and afraid — is compromised by parents who are unable to tolerate the idea that their children have feelings separate from them. Many worry that they may be failing if their children don't see the world through a similar lens.

Children must have opportunities that help them express feelings of their own in order to navigate their world. The expression of authentic feelings, fully felt, helps us know who we are so that we can become our own best authority. And children need to be able to confidently articulate a sense of "I" before they can successfully engage in the experience of "We."

Once Sarah's parents saw that their daughter's difficulties, her isolation and outbursts, were rooted in her inability to safely express her feelings to them, they became committed to understanding and encouraging greater emotional openness.

What You Resist Will Persist

Instead of trying to get Sarah to "behave," they started to watch her behavior for clues; and they became adept at figuring out what emotion she was trying to express in each episode. The silly, the annoying, the seemingly mundane issues that they had been trying to minimize took on new meaning. Scratchy socks became an chance to express frustration and anger over not feeling comfortable. Monsters in the closet and the need for a night light provided an opportunity to verbalize fear. Losing a stuffed animal that had not been played with in years was now respected as a reason for sadness. Silliness was a way to express joy and happiness. As the father joked,"Kids are like sloppy robbers, they leave clues everywhere."

Once Sarah began to trust that she could safely express her feelings to her parents, life at home and school quickly began to improve. Emotional outbursts became less frequent; and her willfulness became less of a problem when her parents discovered that they could engage her cooperation more quickly by mirroring what she was feeling than by squelching such expression. At school, her greater comfort with the expression of feelings, her own and others', enabled her to form friendships with other children, to be become comfortable with the "we," and to develop a social life.

For Sarah's father in particular, his daughter's reversal was a double triumph. Not only was he able to restore her to a path of healthy emotional growth, but in acquiring the skills of empathy, he learned something about himself and his own childhood. Looking for clues in children does not come naturally to parents who as children were "seen and not heard." This father thought that he was being wise by trying to talk Sarah out of her feelings; but it left him ill-prepared to just listen. He came to realize that he need not agree with Sarah's statements about her life, that it was enough for him to allow her to use those statements as emotional self-expression. And in learning to just listen, he came to better understand his child as she grew, and so strengthen the parent-child bond that he could treasure for the rest of his life.

The Need to Tolerate Ambivalence

When I met seven-year-old Ryan and his mother, I knew from a prior phone conversation that I would likely be the last therapist they would see, since she and her husband were considering residential placement for their son. Her look of hopelessness as she entered my office broke my heart.

Ryan was an adorable boy, full of chaotic energy. He burst into my playroom and immediately bombarded me with questions. After a few minutes of frantic exploration, he asked if I had any guns he could play with. Not stopping for an answer, he then started to throw the life-size golden-retriever puppet into the air. His mother tried to settle him down to no avail while I began to narrate his experience. I told him that the playroom was a place where he could say and do almost anything, except destroy the toys, or hurt himself, his mother, or me. After a moment of puzzlement, he broke into a mischievous smile and resumed throwing the dog-puppet around the room. To help him, I set the boundaries: I told him that I would let him know if anything he was doing was unacceptable. He acknowledged my instructions with a quick "OK."

Mom was relieved at this quick rapport with her son, and she opened up to tell me their history. While he continued to whirl around the room, stopping occasionally to forcefully bump into his mother, she told me that her son's obsession with guns and violence was getting him into trouble both at school and home. He intimidated the other children, and was rarely invited for playdates.

Ryan shifted his focus to the "rain stick" propped in a corner, which he quickly transformed into an imaginary gun. Mom stiffened, but I entered the play with him by asking what he would do with the gun. He responded by shooting the retriever puppet, mimicking bullet sounds. Dispassionately, I narrated his story as he killed off several puppets and his mother. Both mother and son seemed surprised that I wasn't distressed by his "acting out." But my acceptance of his play within the boundaries I had established enabled us to understand without judgment what guns meant to him.

His parents, an older couple, had trouble conceiving and were thrilled to finally have a son. Both had been parented in a conventional "spare the rod, spoil the child" way and were determined to not discipline their child similarly. But as the boy turned three, his normal aggression triggered memories of harsh physical punishment in his parents and left them frozen as to how to react. They tried their best to talk him out of his feelings and squelch his actions, which did nothing but temporarily drive them underground. His behavior became more and more exaggerated; and by the time he reached pre-school, his violent acting out was a dominant theme.

Feeling helpless, these worried parents took their son to his first therapist when he was three. Her method was to work alone with Ryan and spend little time talking to and learning about the parents. Her own worry about Ryan's aggression led her to recommend medication to help with his behavior. This "help" first came in the form of Ritalin, which after a year had not helped at all. Various other anti-psychotic drugs followed over the next few years; they caused many negative side effects but did not eliminate his obsession with violence.

By the time Ryan's parents found me, they had been through a four-year journey of frustration and medication, following the advice of experts who told them nothing about the normal developmental milestones of a boy of Ryan's age.

To me this was a clear case of "what you resist will persist." No one had attempted to understand in a non-judgmental way what the violence meant to Ryan; instead, everyone worked to squelch, to resist, his anti-social behavior. And so, without an empathic understanding, the behavior persisted.

During the early treatment sessions, I played with Ryan with a parent present in the room. For several weeks, we enacted the same scene, which he directed with passion and skill. I was told to sit on the floor; then he would "kill" me by shooting me down. When I asked what I should do next, he would giggle, tell me I was dead, and then have me come back to life in order to repeat the scene. Over and over, I would hit the ground and then pop up enthusiastically, alive and well. The more dramatic I was, the more calm he became. He was clearly enchanted by his power to get rid of me and then bring me back to life. And by acting out his feelings in a safe, responsive environment, he could make sense of them. After a while Ryan became bored with this game and began to use other toys in the playroom, almost always creating and expressing themes of power and control, with his parents and me as empathic witnesses.

After a couple of months, his play evolved; he began to seek out toys that would demonstrate skills and mastery. His use of the playroom was no longer frantic, just exploratory; and he clearly enjoyed showing off what he could achieve. It was during this period that Ryan began to share feelings about how much he loved his mother. In one session when he and I were working alone, he asked if we could go into my adjoining office and "just talk." He was fascinated with my psychoanalytic-ally-inspired fainting couch, on which he immediately performed some mini gymnastics. Afterward he settled on the two seater and asked if we could talk about his father. He told me that while he loved his father, who was "awesome," he was also afraid of him. In the quiet that followed, I took the opportunity to tell him how normal it is for kids to both love and hate their parents. This perplexed him. I asked his permission to sit next to him. Once side by side, I pulled out a notebook in which I drew a simple Venn diagram, two circles that overlapped in the middle. In one circle I wrote, "I HATE DAD"; in the other, I wrote, "I LOVE DAD." I pointed to the overlapping space in between and said, "See how loving and hating are happening at the same time?" He gave me his Ryan-grin and went back to his gymnastics on the fainting couch.

At the end of the session, I wasn't sure if I had gotten through to this medicated, seven-year-old boy with my Venn-diagram explanation of ambivalence. But a story I heard from his mother in the next session told me that he had understood it quite well. Ryan ran to his mom during a playdate, complaining and clearly annoyed at his friend whom he had invited over. When his mother asked if he wanted the friend to go home, he created a circle with the thumb and forefinger of each hand, two circles together that overlapped in the middle, and spoke his frustration, "I want him to go home, I want him to stay!" And with that, he went back to his friend to work through their differences.

As the story of Ryan reveals, it is stunning to see how quickly and easily children can be helped with their behavior. By contrast, the dependence on mind-altering drugs can be devastating to a young child who needs to make sense out of his (or her) feelings while building inner resources. Ryan was a normally aggressive boy who was acting out his feelings of ambivalence, especially toward his father, during a very tender age. (See *The Incredible Oedipal.*) The medication did very little to help him sort out his emotions so that he could "put them into words." What the medication did was to make his normal developmental issues more difficult to identify. People around him misunderstood his need to turn aggression into assertion, and so they tried to eliminate the behavior without understanding it. His behavior had become more troubling over time as he got older.

What helped Ryan was simple play-therapy, an empathic therapeutic environment where the behavior was accepted rather than resisted, with the inclusion of his parents so that they could understand the ghosts that had left the nursery and taken up residence in their home.

Optimal Frustrations

Living, by necessity, involves delay between desire and fulfillment, between plan and realization. In other words, it involves frustration and the endurance of frustration.

— Haim Ginott

I took an oath during my pregnancy that I would be the kindest, smartest, and most loving mother ever. For nine months, I prepared by reading as many child development books as I could, feeling satisfaction every time I came across a theory that supported my need to "not do to my child what was done to me." It was the early 80s; and like many at the time I was awed by such authors as Brazelton, Ginott, and Fraiberg as well as the parenting series from the Gesell Institute. These parenting experts became my first "idealizing figures." At the time I was also completing a Master's degree in Mental Health Counseling, in which I was studying the impact of early childhood experiences on adult mental health. I was devoted to "getting it right" in order to both have a healing experience for me and ensure the future success and happiness of my child.

And as it turned out, I was the best parent ever — until I actually became one.

Struggling to Become a Parent
While Feeling like a Child

Was I shocked! With the best intentions, once my child was born, my fantasy of blissful perfection met the reality of caring for an infant. My days soon became filled with conflicts and challenges that left me exhausted by the five o'clock "witching hour." It was then that my baby regularly became fussy, which brought up in me feelings of failure. And I became dependent on others' parenting advice that I passionately did not want.

At times I felt like a child myself whose "new," bright ideas about parenting fell short of what I expected and left me vulnerable to the "conventional wisdom" I was rebelling against. I still remember the humiliation of my adorable child's first public temper tantrum.

In response, I dug deeper into my books and came to a new understanding of the importance of a child's experience of frustration. What I learned is that our human failings as parents and the frustration they produce in children are essential for their growth.

When I See You, I See Me

My research helped me to understand the natural flood and ebb of early parental responsiveness and how the parents' inevitable failures trigger in children frustration and the need to endure it. As D. W. Winicott explains in *Babies and Their Mothers*, "ordinarily the woman enters into a phase, a phase from which she ordinarily recovers in the weeks and months after the baby's birth, in which to a large extent she is the baby and the baby is her." In this period of "maternal preoccupation" the mother becomes heavily invested in satisfying the needs of her dependent infant, "relying upon memories of being cared for, which either help or hinder her in her own experiences as a mother." Feeling as "one with a baby" contributes to a natural knowing about when the baby needs to be held, fed and changed. According to Winicott, this illusion of oneness allows the baby "to be, out of which there can arise the next things that have to do with action, doing and being done to."

Eventually, as the "maternal preoccupation" with the infant naturally fades, the mother begins to refocus on her own needs. This important shift between mother and child ushers in a process of separation/individuation which will last into early adulthood. It is at the outset of this journey that the baby begins to experience a "self" that is real, subject to disappointments, and being let down by the person they most depend upon. During the child's first twenty-one years, indeed over their lifetime, the mother and child will choreograph their unique relationship dance. To the extent that they see the other in themselves, it is highly probable that each will always influence the other's thinking and doing. It is because of their mutual influence that a mother is uniquely qualified to respond to a child's frustrations in an optimal way. Later on, other caregivers can and will be as instrumental in helping the child in this important task.

NO!

As all parents know, children are easy to disappoint. We let them down without ever having to try, often to our utter surprise. And yet from frustration is born frustration tolerance — the frustration as they wait to be picked up and held, as hunger builds, as bare bottoms stay soiled. Over time tolerance becomes more complicated as they venture out to become their own people, able to finally do for themselves. Each stage of development presents opportunities to feel conflicted over going along with or going ahead independently. It is essential for humans to think and to do for themselves since it is the primary way we develop our skills and lifelong talents.

Children, especially in toddlerhood, begin to build their separate self by saying "no" to something or someone. Yet as our children begin to say "no," our own memories of being denied this privilege are reactivated. Children's defiance can bring back awful memories for the parents who are trying their best to get them to cooperate. A simple "no" can turn a morning into a drama of disappointments, leaving everyone, including Mom and Dad, in tears.

I Want, I Need

Michael's mom began the session complaining bitterly about her young son's lack of frustration-tolerance. It was getting him into trouble in and out of school. His teacher complained that he always had to have the last word and that he felt that the classroom rules were "unfair." His winning or losing each game at recess would dictate his mood for the rest of the afternoon, and his classmates were becoming increasingly annoyed at his bad sportsmanship. Michael's sense of "I" was not strong and was preventing him from being part of the "we"; and his parents' dismay and lack of understanding did not improve the situation.

In a session with the parents, I learned that both of them had been raised in traditional households with autocratic rules. Michael's mom remembered this part of her childhood with discomfort, but the father reminisced wistfully. When I asked how they reconciled this difference between them, the mom confessed that it was frustrating that he did not understand child development; for his part, he praised the "good old days when kids knew their place."

What I saw was that each parent was unconsciously acting out their individual childhood conflicts: the mother didn't want her son to feel the pain of having his wishes denied while the dad was taking the control denied to him as a child. In practice, Mom met all her sons needs quickly while Dad automatically said "no" to his son's requests, which were later re-negotiated in a heated battle between husband and wife. As a result, Michael got many of his needs met but learned that there would always be a protracted struggle involved.

Such a common family dynamic doesn't allow for a child to develop the skills needed to delay gratification and cope with disappointment. In Michael's case, every time his needs became a parental battle, he lost the opportunity to use his own inner resources. Michael felt like he could never "win" because the debate was always between the parents; and he came to see life as "unfair" because "what Mom gave, Dad could take away."

Although initially resistant, the father came to realize that his fear of "spoiling" his son was creating a child who fell apart every time things were not to his satisfaction. As the father's harsh approach softened, the mother felt less of a need to be her son's protector.

New ways of communication helped this family. I encouraged them to use a "two step" process when responding to Michael's wants and needs. When he wanted to do something unsafe or inappropriate, his parents learned to first react with empathy before dissuading him. In addition, instead of relying on "because I said so," Michael's father spoke to his son in a way that showed respect for his child's wishes; and Mom, rather than immediately gratify her son, became adept at finding appropriate substitutes to help Michael accept delayed gratification. For his part, the son felt rewarded in the praise he received from both parents in his growing ability to cope.

In one example of Michael's growth, as happily reported by his mother, he approached her in the kitchen while she was cooking dinner for him and a playmate. He insisted on cookies for himself and his friend. Acknowledging his craving, she told him that he could not have cookies before dinner. This triggered an angry outburst that lasted several minutes; but then her son went quiet for a minute and said, "OK Mom, can we have carrot sticks instead? I can get them myself." By the time we reached this point in the treatment, both Michael's mom and I felt that he was well on his way to managing his frustrations and developing his own resources to gain power and control.

In *Helping Young Children Grow*, Erna Furman writes,

> Learning to cope with frustrations works best when the frustration is manageable, when it produces the kind of hardship a child can bear by mustering his own resources. In this sense it is similar to building up bodily strength. A good exercise program gauges the right number of push-ups to start with and increases them gradually. We would feel some discomfort each time but, as our muscles toughen, we could tackle even harder tasks... It is the parent's job to gauge the 'exercise program,' to gauge what kind of frustration the youngster can handle, and when and how.

Later, you will learn how coping with frustration is different for each stage of development.

Feeling Grand: Being Expansive

Have you ever felt like you were a little bit different? Like you had something unique to offer the world, if you could just get people to see it? Then you know exactly how it feels to be me!

— Flint in *Cloudy With A Chance of Meatballs*, 2009

All children are born with a unique set of talents and abilities, what I call the individual blueprint. If caregivers respond to this blueprint adequately, the child will feel a sense of expansiveness that will help him or her use this plan to achieve personal goals over a lifetime.

Children need to feel significant and competent as they grow in order to reach for what their parents have; their everyday experiences become opportunities to learn what it means to take initiative in the world. Imagine a child taking her first steps; this is an early experience of expansiveness that is both exciting and scary. This watershed moment and how it is responded to will influence how the child will deal with the excitement and fear of future expansive moments — such as running down the hall alone, crawling inside an open closet, or chasing the cat behind the sofa.

How parents react to such thrilling adventures can either encourage or inhibit future initiative-taking. Some parents allow too much freedom while other parents are tense with worry as their own needs and memories get in the way of allowing their children to just be themselves in a safe environment. It can be hard to know whether you are allowing your child to show you what only they know about who they wish to be. But as it turns out, there is something you can do about this, and it will not be as hard as you think! Join me as we watch and listen to three mothers at a local playground.

It's a Jungle Gym Out There

Several mothers and their children are enjoying the morning at a playground. The jungle gym is the preferred activity, engaging the children as the mothers talk nearby. One very determined child struggles to the top and then turns around to find his mother. With a big grin on his face he shouts, "Look at me!" The boy's mom, deep in conversation with a friend, did not hear him until his third try. "Mom. Mommy. Look at me! " Her attention finally caught, the mother is annoyed at the interruption. Her response is deadening, "What do you want? Get down now. You will hurt yourself up there." She turns back to her friend and complains that her son is always getting injured.

Another mother, using this moment as a stage to get her own needs met, encourages her child to climb higher. He insists that he is afraid. "Don't be a fraidy cat, you can do it," she says impatiently. The child reaches the top, tense and worried. His mother is buoyant, exclaiming, "There you go. I told you you could do it. I am so proud of you!"

Minutes later, a third child reaches the top of the jungle gym. Her mother has been watching her gradual ascent and waits patiently until her daughter turns to find her mother's face below. Mom's face has little expression until her beaming daughter shouts, "Look at me!" Mom's face now changes to reflect her daughter's enthusiasm, "Yes, I see. You really feel great up there. You are so proud of yourself!"

Look at Me, Look at Me

What we just heard and observed were three different reactions to children in the process of exploring their emerging talent and ability. Each "securely attached child," as I explain the term in *The Mighty Milestones*, was eager to have an audience for an adventure where they could feel quite grand, and express their excitement. Each mother's response defined the expansive experience for the child.

Our first mother did not realize the importance of her son's climb to the top of the jungle gym and so missed an opportunity to mirror his thrill of achievement. Here, the mother and child were intent on using playtime in different ways: Mom wanted time to chat with her friend, and the son wanted to show off his ability. This situation and the result are quite common. Most parents have not been taught to use play as an opportunity to cement in feelings of expansiveness and competence. Instead, they use it to have some badly needed free time for themselves. This mother did not realize that she was squelching her son's natural need for a supportive audience because she needed an audience, the audience of her friend.

The second mother had a different agenda that also prevented her from understanding her child's need to explore and achieve. Her investment in his success was so strong that she was willing to bully him beyond his comfort zone. So he learned that taking initiative is worrisome especially if your audience wants you to do more than you are ready for. His attempt to please his beloved parent brought a humiliating response, "Don't be a fraidy cat." The emotional price paid to avoid disappointing her was large, and probably she was the only one feeling proud and accomplished that morning.

Our third mom instinctively seemed to know just what her daughter needed: the opportunity to show her what she could do. The mother's face remained serene as she waited to see how her daughter was feeling as she was climbing the jungle gym. She did not interfere; she provided a secure base, available when her daughter needed her. Mom's attitude made it possible for her to reach the top at her own pace. Once there, the child sought out her mother among the crowd and beamed down enthusiasm and joy. It was then that the mother reflected back her child's feelings of grandiosity.

The jungle gym is just one of the many places where children meet their essential need to demonstrate mastery and control, feelings that are only made real by an appropriate response from the caregiver.

The Invisible Secure Base

A child needs the parent both to provide the secure emotional base and to mirror the experience of adventure and exploration. There are many ways that caregivers build a secure base for their children. As we have discussed, these include letting them have all their feelings and helping them to tolerate ambivalence and frustration.

Children alternate in their expressed need for their secure base and their need for their caregiver's reflection of grand feelings, but they can only internalize their adventures if they trust that their secure base is present. The reason that children value your mirroring so highly is that in their moments of exploration, they know, through your presence, that they will not be alone with their feelings.

You may already have experienced your child's need for mirroring of grandiosity through such statements as, "Watch me, watch me. I jump rope better when you are watching," and "Dad, what's the point of me doing it if you are not there." With each exclamation comes the child's longing to be accurately mirrored — but not too much, and not too little, as Goldilocks would say, "just right."

Goldilocks Revisited

My young patient Alex was a grade-school student with a beautiful singing voice. His well meaning parents and doting grandparents were overly invested in his early success, not to mention their great ambitions for him as the family fell captive to the adoration of their small community.

The bubble burst during a first-grade school recital when Alex said he could no longer be on stage. He ran to the bathroom and vomited and was unable to join his classmates. His parents assured him that this was normal performance anxiety and that he would feel better in no time, but his anxiety persisted. Within several weeks his fear of being on stage spread to a fear of even going to school. His parents kept telling him how great he was and how everyone missed him, but this did nothing to soothe his anxiety.

I chose to work with Alex through child-centered play therapy. Initially his play was unfocussed; but after several weeks Alex became more confident in deciding how to use his time. He began to express his anger about always being told when and what to do at home and at school. He opened up about how he used to love to perform, but that now he hated it, and that what he hated most was his mother's face as she sat in the audience. He felt like she was always "smiling too hard" when she was watching him; he didn't want to see her excitement when he performed.

The case of Alex is a wonderful illustration of a child whose grandiose experience could not be his own because of his parents own thwarted needs for mirroring. Alex had become an agent for his mother's success; and when she took his success for herself, she took away his secure base, which he needed in order to explore his emerging artistic talent.

With an understanding of what Alex needed in order to continue his exploration, his parents realized that they had to establish a secure base according to his definition. So that he could return to the stage with his classmates, his mother promised that she would sit in the back of the audience without smiling. She and her husband stopped talking about his brilliant future. They listened to *him* tell *them* how he felt when performing, and they supported his experimental, sometimes silly ideas that gave him pleasure. School performances once again became a great adventure rather than just a pursuit of excellence that brought him praise and attention. In the end, the mother and the rest of the family learned how their smiling responses must be not too much, not too little, but just right!

More books to read!

Your Child's Self-Esteem, by Dorothy Briggs.

The Irreducible Needs of Children: What Every Child Must Have To Grow, Learn and Flourish, by T. Berry Brazelton and Stanley Greenspan.

Your Growing Child: From Babyhood Through Adolescence, by Penelope Leach.

How To Talk To Kids So Kids Will Listen, and Listen So That They Will Talk, by Adele Faber & Elaine Mazlish.

Part Three

Caregivers: The Absolutely Essential Relationships

In Memory of Those Parents
Lost on 9/11

Unforgettable: The Enduring Spirit of the Lost Father

By late afternoon on Tuesday September 11, 2001, I knew that my work as a psychotherapist would take on a very new meaning. Calls from frightened patients were coming in fast, leaving me very little time to process my own reaction to what had happened. The destruction of the Twin Towers had made the "ordinary problems of living" a distant memory. My community was now facing the loss of beloved parents and children to a tragic event that in the past would only have occurred in one's imagination.

We all needed to reorganize our mental lives; as a therapist I needed to validate individual reactions while providing hope and optimism. I remember feeling as if I had been caught in a wicked snowstorm, unable to dig out from all the white powdery fear that made it hard to think about anything but survival.

Months went by as the community continued to make sense out of the losses and did its best to help those who had taken the heaviest blows. Relationships became the new affluence in my well-resourced town. We were all heartbroken — for ourselves as well as each other. And then there was Jolie.

Seven-year-old Jolie entered the playroom with the unique agility of a budding gymnast. Her demeanor was a combination of quiet curiosity and impish tentativeness. Long hair pulled back in an elegant ponytail revealed a beautifully open face capable of expressing a wide range of emotions within a span of minutes. As she scanned the room with her signature wide-eyed enthusiasm, her gaze stopped at the corner of the room where the lavender hula-hoops waited precariously for a pair of willing hips. A quick smile covered her face; I thought of a butterfly before flight.

Months of previous work had enabled us to assemble the stage quickly. She was ready for another performance, certain that I would be a willing and interested partner in the play. Looking a bit like a fresh-faced cheerleader, Jolie proudly assumed her position on our impromptu stage, demurely announcing her intentions. All of us, especially the life-sized golden retriever and twin monkey puppets, waited in anticipation.

I sat and watched as Jolie's youthful energy was transformed into minutes of spell-binding hula-hooping, hoping to capture and understand her momentary experience of intoxicating competence. Her face, radiant, grew soft as the show ended. She sat next to me as we listened to the beads inside the hoops cascade together, quieting down like a festive crowd after the show.

I narrated her experience back to her; this sparked a new demonstration of skill as she jumped up and hurled a hoop across the room. Like a ballet dancer leaping across the stage, her hoop flew into the air in graceful abandonment. Over and over, we watched and followed the final destination of her efforts. Soon, she became quite adept at being able to control the hoop with a certain flick of the wrist. She gleefully expressed pride in what she could accomplish. Then her face changed again as she stopped and sat on one of the child-sized playroom chairs.

We sat across from one another. I knew from the intensity in her face that her next words would be important. Slowly Jolie explained that her father had taught her that trick with the hula hoop but that she had never had a chance to show him. The child of a deeply spiritual family, Jolie then verbalized their belief, "Dad is always looking down at me from heaven, he is always present!" This statement comforted us both. She continued, "I know he is here, right? He can see me now." My reply, prompted by instinct and wonder, attempted to both capture and expand her experience, "And now we are both here watching you."

Helping Jolie keep the memory of her father alive was essential for her growth and development. Described as a wonderful mentor who had always encouraged adventure, Dad was often the one she would go to when she was feeling most expansive. I understood the importance of this relationship and worked to re-connect her developmental strivings that were quickly disappearing inside the traumatized family milieu. Over time her mother become more able to understand and respond to Jolie's playfulness; this brought back some joy and optimism to this emotionally depleted family. The mother also did her best to identify other family and friends who could step in and reinforce what we had accomplished in the playroom.

People Who Need People

Those of us who worked with and documented the challenges of Tuesday's Children, the children of parents lost in 9/11, were painfully aware of how the loss of important relationships continually impacted their growth and development. The "absolutely essential needs" of these children were totally disrupted as their families did their best to survive the tragedy. The need to find surrogate figures highlighted the importance of experiences that could only be had with another person.

These experiences not only promoted healing; but as in the case of Jolie, they helped to get these kids back onto the track of their healthy development.

My work with the families of 9/11 became an opportunity to focus on ways to teach others about the essential needs of children and the responses needed from caregivers. I found what worked best: an approach that unified child development theories and my training in psychoanalytic psychotherapy. Ironically, were it not for the crime that ripped apart these families, they might not have ever sought treatment. But ripped apart they were, and the need for parental efficacy was crucial.

This is some of what we all learned albeit in exaggerated circumstances.

Adults with Empathy

It was that Tuesday morning. Devin was finally settling into his morning routine at school. His eight-year-old brain and body were focused on behaving in class and paying attention to his teacher. It was life as usual for this spirited child, who found it challenging to just sit still and listen. He had learned his lessons well: to be quiet, to respect classroom order, and to be a good school citizen. Turning his freckled face toward his buddy Jared, he tried to make him giggle and hoped that they wouldn't get into trouble. As Devin had gotten better at following classroom rules, the new school year had gotten off to a good start. And just that morning he had promised his father to keep it that way.

But before noon, Devin was being driven home by a trusted neighbor who had no idea how to prepare him for the chaos ahead.

Knowing that something was terribly wrong, Devin frantically searched for his mother as soon as he got into the house. He was greeted by his grandparents, who looked worried; he knew his grandmother had been crying because she had mascara bunched up all around her eyes.

He kept asking for his mother, all the while trying to make sense of the new energy in his house. Grandma and Grandpa seemed anxious to keep him out of the family room, where he could hear the sounds of the television and the quiet sobbing from someone who sounded like his mother. Using all his might, he pushed pass Grandpa and ran to his crying mother, where he saw for the first time what she had been watching all morning: a burning building that looked like the one where his dad worked. He had been there just last summer.

It was that awesome building, one of a pair, as awesome as his dad.

Devin was just one of the over-three-thousand children who were traumatized by 9/11. Their blueprints had been stomped on and crumpled by circumstances beyond their control. I knew it would be hard to restore what had been taken away from them; and as it turned out, adults with empathy provided essential relationships for the children and parents with whom I worked. It was painful to listen to their fear, anger, and profound sadness. Many, many tears were shed in my office, some by the children, others by the parents, and some by me.

Together we stayed in the pain that none of us could run from. The tears and rage were respected and understood. I refused the "conventional wisdom" which encouraged them to move on. Eventually, everyone started to create new lives; and the children started to play again. It turned out that being understood made life bearable and worth living. Empathy is where it all began.

This section is devoted to the absolutely essential relationships between children and their primary caregivers. The responsiveness of the caregiver will either satisfy or frustrate an innate human emotional need. And emotional development throughout life depends on the healthy satisfaction of these needs, which will be described as Idealizing, Mirroring, Twinship and Adversarial. These concepts are part of the framework of Self Psychology, founded by Heinz Kohut.

I will be explaining this process through the story of Devin. He didn't lose his father in an accident; he lost him in the exaggerated circumstances of 9/11. Devin's status as the victim of an international crime which occupied the news for years afterward delayed his healing. As the family therapist I pointed out to his mother, who was dealing with her own shock and grief, the importance of fostering relationships with alternate caregivers so that her son would seek to get his essential needs met, thus returning him to a more normal path of emotional growth.

Devin had grown up in a healthy family where his essential needs were satisfied and where the essential relationships were established in his early childhood development, as I will explain in *The Mighty Milestones*. His story demonstrates how even in a healthy family trauma can wipe out developmental accomplishments, but which can be restored with careful attention.

Mergers and Acquisitions: Idealizing

Devin and his father had been great pals who spent a lot of time together outdoors on weekends. They both possessed a high degree of kinesthetic intelligence (to be addressed in *School Daze)*, which is why the father understood how hard it was for him to sit still in a classroom all day.

Devin looked up to his father; he respected his Dad's opinion and thought that he was really smart. Whenever he had a problem in school or with his brother he would seek his father's advice, which made everything more manageable. He was using their relationship to have an "idealizing experience": being merged with and accepted by a strong, calm and wise protective figure that possessed admirable qualities that he still lacked. Devin was internalizing the ego strength of his father, helping the development of his self-control and ability to tolerate frustration and disappointment; at least he was until that Tuesday morning when his world went up in smoke, leaving only ashes and memories.

The Tragedy of Unmet Potential

Devin and his brother slept with their mother for weeks, unable to shed their feelings of panic and fear. They all waited for the phone call that would release them from their misery, an elated voice announcing that their father had been found out there somewhere, wounded but alive. Each day the children would return from school and search their mother's face for signs of a miracle; each day their hopeful feelings sank into despair. The father was never heard from or seen again, and for these young boys his disappearance was developmentally incomprehensible.

Devin's mother carried on as best she could. She got the children to school, met the demands of her job, and allowed her extended family to help with her sons. She entered my practice for much needed support, and together we met the challenges of this uncommon tragedy.

It took years before this mother would feel safe again. The children benefited tremendously from her ability to recreate a "secure base." They were feeling better about leaving the nest that had been so lovingly repaired, and she became more social. It was when we thought everyone's development was back on track that Devin began having real problems at home and school as his needs for expansiveness created a renewed need for his father.

School was no longer the safe haven it had been immediately after 9/11. The passing of years had made his teachers less compassionate, and at times he found himself in lectures about 9/11 that only served to reopen his wounds. Devin tried really hard to "act like a man," which to him meant that instead of talking out his feelings he acted them out. His "inappropriate and unacceptable behavior" was increasing in a school environment of diminishing empathy.

At home Devin was more quiet than usual and was less interested in shooting hoops or inviting over friends. One evening as the mother began her normal routine of homework checking and bedtime negotiations, she encountered the shock of being unable to find her son. After searching everywhere inside and outside the house, she heard her younger son calling from Devin's bedroom. Entering the room, her heart sank as she saw the tightly curled body of her son lying on his bed, covered in a early childhood quilt. Sitting down next to him, she saw that his face was bloated from crying. When she asked him what was wrong, all he could say was, "I can't."

Hide and Seek

Devin's disappearing act became the template he would use for several years as he struggled to make sense of his feelings. As he grew older, he wandered farther, prompting frantic phone calls to neighbors and relatives that began a search that would last well into the night and sometimes early morning. Curiously he always picked a safe destination and one where he could be found. After receiving his first cell phone, the game of hide and seek took on a new dimension, enabling him to reach out to his mother when he wanted rescue.

His mother and I came to understand the significance of his running away; Devin needed the experience of hiding and knowing that others would try to find him. The involvement of his friends and family reminded him how valuable he was and how important his safety was to them.

Devin was acting out an important issue that begged for an empathic response. He was unconsciously recreating his father's disappearance over and over; only now he was in control of the ending. Normal adolescent exploratory needs were becoming more distorted as he began to take more risks with himself and family property. Themes of destruction and loss were now a part of everyday family life as were the conventional responses of his school and home, which failed to control him. The spirited, freckle-faced kid had become just like one of those on the ubiquitous street fliers after 9/11: a beautiful person gone missing.

Talk It Out or Act It Out

Given the symbolic importance of his behavior, I rejected the notion that his family wasn't being "hard enough" on him. My real concern was that we would lose him to an accident before the steady, empathic, adult attention would reach him. His mother gently began to share with him what she and I thought might be going on. His response was unremarkable although he did sit and listen. His risky behavior continued, but it became less frequent. Eventually, he started going through the old family albums and explored the 9/11 websites, which honored his father and others who had been lost.

One evening, in a homework battle with his mom, he screamed, "I wish you had been in that building, not him." As they cried together, she held him in her arms and told him how much she understood that he needed and missed his buddy.

He started shooting hoops again.

Ain't You Grand: Mirroring

Driveway basketball became a healthy habit, enabling Devin to burn off energy and keep it together in class. A family friend who also loved the sport installed a new hoop for him and would play regularly, showering the young talent with genuine compliments.

As the leaves on the trees were turning, this young man's attention turned to all things basketball. His obsession with 9/11 stories faded, replaced by basketball heroes and their stories. When his anxious mother reported this new obsession and his talking about the greatness of certain players, I explained that in this reparative "idealizing experience" his identification with these basketball stars was important for his rapidly developing skills.

At my encouragement she starting reading alongside him during his hero-worship sessions so that she could reflect his excitement back to him. Closely watching his facial expressions, she narrated what she thought he was feeling so that he would be comfortable expanding on those thoughts and feelings. She patiently validated the importance of these heroes to her son. With time her efforts were rewarded as he seemed lighter and more playful afterward.

With the emotional foundation established by his mother he took the risk and tried out for the middle school basketball team. To the delight to his extended family he made the team, which introduced him to his next "idealizing figure," his coach.

Coach Joe was thrilled to have a real talent like Devin on the team. And while he was in awe of this young player's energy and skill, he did not like his foul language and disrespect for the practice schedule. And here the coach gave Devin just what he needed: positive mirroring and firm boundaries.

Basketball provided Devin an ideal opportunity to satisfy his "exhibitionist and grandiose needs." He knew that his strong and powerful coach would always keep him in line, allowing him to show off his skills appropriately. After each basket Devin looked for Joe's face, for that certain gleam in his coach's eyes that made him want to do more even after disappointments and frustrations on the court.

For his friends and family, the weekend games were a joyful ritual. But while Devin loved the attention, he would sometimes act out so terribly that his loyal following would leave early or stop coming.

The Tango of Desire and Resistance

As with many traumatized children and adults, there comes a time when the "restoration of the self" creates fear and ambivalence. The acceptance of admiration can be scary especially after it has been crushed as profoundly as it had been for Devin. While it seemed ridiculous to others, it made sense to me that Devin was rejecting the gratification of his essential needs. He was terrified of being re-injured at a time when he was finally feeling expansive. Feeling grand had became reminiscent of those magical times spent with his father; but he was afraid of enjoying the mirroring response only to lose it again. And so he would reject it before it could be taken from him.

Once again Devin's Mom was receiving a lot of conventional wisdom from those as perplexed as she was. Some thought that he should be "disciplined" by taking away his sports altogether;

but she trusted me to let patient empathy work its magic. The constant, special attention of Devin's mom and his coach enabled him to work through his insecurity and ambivalence and helped the bewildered extended family to continue supporting him.

To Know Me Is to Love Me

This tango was exhausting; but we all became better dancers as Devin continued to grow. His need to disappear had changed into a need to show himself off both in school and out. He was accepting the praise for his athletic ability and even became boastful; this star athlete was finally accepting the inheritance of his father's good looks and charm. Having been raised in a family that considered "modesty the best policy," Devin's mom worried about her son's conceit. I explained to her that her son's grandiosity was "touch-up work," which I will address in *Kitchen-Table Therapy,* and that he was developing parts of himself that had gone underground after the death of his father.

Empathy provided her with the essential tools she needed to validate his feelings of omnipotence and grandeur. She understood that Devin's acceptance of his own greatness was essential to his development, and she found ways to validate his feelings while helping him to express them in socially appropriate ways. In time his vanity matured into a need for healthy recognition.

Just Like Me: Twinship

Devin's popularity continued on and off the basketball court, and he continued to attract many new friends. One particular boy, Joshua, shared Devin's inclination towards classroom mischief and an ambition to be a professional athlete. Josh's life had also been torn apart, in his case by the recent divorce of his parents. In addition to their shared interests, each found comfort in the knowledge that he was not alone in his loss. Each had a buddy "just like me."

Time spent together in school extended to time spent together at home. Afternoons of shooting hoops in the driveway led to impromptu dinners at Devin's house or Joshua's, and Saturday night sleepovers were a regular occurrence. Devin's mom grew to love the sight of the boys sacked out in the family room on Sunday morning and secretly enjoyed the ritual of rousing them for church with the rest of the family.

The Power of Two

Devin and Josh's "twinship" helped each grow into their individual selves after the disruption to their secure base. The loss that each had suffered set them back in their development and made each of them feel alone in the world. Finding out about each other's shared talent and sense of humor was just what they needed to feel unique and part of the world at the same time.

I Beg to Differ: Adversarial Exchanges

"Without conflict there is no growth," I said to Devin's mom as she adjusted yet again to another phase in her son's touch-up work. The coach had threatened to suspend the two boys from the next game because of their repeated horsing around during practice. In a heated kitchen argument, Devin vented about the "stupid drills" in which Josh and he had to participate even though they didn't help him get ready for a game. This new rupture with the coach brought back Mom's memories of her son's earlier tantrums on the court, which had almost snuffed out what was to become a brilliant high school basketball career. Mom's conventional reaction was to tell him not to question the coach's rules, but this only inflamed Devin's rage. I advised her to encourage Devin to talk through his differences with the coach rather than act them out. If Devin had other drills in mind that would better prepare him for a game, she would work with him to present his ideas to the coach.

It was because Coach Joe had become so important to Devin that he needed to use the coach to satisfy his "adversarial need," the need to have one's feelings and opinions accepted even when they are different. As children grow, they are always preparing for the day when they have to be out on their own. And by the time the child reaches high school, his capacity to function self-sufficiently, to leave his secure base and explore the world out there, depends upon his ability be autonomous. Adversarial exchanges with trusted caregivers are essential to a sense of autonomy.

The coach wisely acknowledged Devin's suggestions and commented that while they might be best for him they didn't serve the whole team. Once Devin's need "to do it his way" was understood by his mother and coach, he found it easier follow the rules, albeit reluctantly.

Devin continued to look to others as he prepared for college. Happily he was able to recognize individuals who could respond to his essential needs in a positive way. Devin began to idealize an older cousin, a college varsity soccer player, who helped Devin achieve similar athletic success.

I have used the story of Devin to demonstrate the absolutely essential relationships, which are important not only in early childhood but throughout a young person's emotional development and even into adulthood. As a primary caregiver, who helps the child fulfill the need for such a relationship, it is important to do so with empathy. Empathizing is listening to another person in such a way that they believe they are being thoroughly understood. Repeated experiences with a primary caregiver of feeling that one's point of view is understood and accepted empower an individual to foster empathic relationships with others where they will expect and provide the same level of understanding that they received in childhood.

Practicing empathy with children, especially when they are acting out their needs, is time consuming and may feel fruitless in the beginning. And an empathic parent will get no support from conventional wisdom, which in all my years of experience doesn't have an ounce of empathy in it. Devin's mom once described this empathic parenting approach as "the road less traveled by." But as we saw with Devin, it works; and it is the only thing that works. It is the mission of this book to teach all parents to trust empathy and in so doing to break out of Parent Fatigue Syndrome, which is the inevitable result of counterproductive conventional wisdom.

After the death of his father, Devin's slow healing process delayed his need for idealization, which was eventually revitalized once his mother had restored a secure base for his brother and him. Thanks to the repeated efforts of his coach, he could once again trust that there could be another person he could look up to, merge with, and whose strengths he could internalize. The eventual acceptance of the appropriate mirroring of his athletic grandeur filled him with a sense of efficacy and ability to take initiative in the world. His friendship with Josh helped him feel that there was someone just like him; he was no longer a weirdo, just someone able to make a unique contribution to his community. And finally, because both his coach and his mother understood his need to have his own opinions accepted, he was able to transform his adversarial exchanges into feelings of sufficient independence and confidence to meet the demands of the world outside his secure base.

At this point in the book, I want you, the reader, to stop reading and step away. When you watch your children, are you seeing whether they are happy, sad, angry or afraid; and are you reflecting their emotions back to them? Are you helping them to understand their moments of ambivalence when they are gripped by genuinely conflicting emotions? Whom do they look up to for strength and wisdom especially during growth spurts? How do they use others to reflect back how wonderful they feel about themselves? Who are their "just like me" friends who provide opportunities for them to feel both unique and part of the world at the same time? Are you respecting their differences of opinion, which are part of their need to feel autonomous?

Your answers to these questions will indicate how well you are meeting your children's essential needs and how well you are recognizing and responding to their essential relationships as they naturally emerge.

When you come back to the book, we will talk about the Mighty Milestones, which occur in the first five years of life. You will discover how these normal developmental stages provide abundant opportunities for children to engage in the essential relationships and the essential experiences that are needed for growth.

More books to read!

Between Parent and Child, by Haim Ginott.

Between Parent and Teenager, by Haim Ginott.

Becoming Attached: Unfolding the Mystery of the Infant-Mother Bond and Its Impact on Later Life, by Robert Karen.

Fatherneed : Why Father Care Is as Essential as Mother Care for Your Child, by Kyle Pruett, M.D.

Get Out Of My Life: but first could you drive me & cheryl to the mall: A Parent's Guide To The New Teenager, by Anthony Wolf, Ph.D.

Siblings Without Rivalry: How To Help Your Children Live Together So That You Can Too, by Adele Faber and Elaine Mazlish.

Part Four

The Mighty Milestones

Becoming Attached

Hold a baby to your ear
As you would a shell:
Sounds of centuries you will hear
New centuries foretell.

Who can break a baby's code?
And which is the older-
The listener or his small load?
The held or the holder?

— E. B. White

Here I sit on my birthday overlooking the city of San Francisco from the bay window of my hotel room, captivated by the fog that envelopes everything but the rooftops of the Victorian beauties outside. At home on Long Island, my family and neighbors are bracing for Hurricane Sandy, whose description as an "unprecedented event" makes it impossible to be prepared, especially emotionally prepared.

For myself, I am trying to come to grips with the idea that my secure base, my home for over 30 years, may not be able to withstand the battering of wind and rain that is predicted. I am trying to stay calm as I imagine what I might see on my return – a changed landscape perhaps and storm damage anywhere from a few fallen branches to total devastation.

I tell myself I have to let go and hope for the best. I am powerless to do anything but pray that mother nature will be kind as she continues to balance the earth's energies that bind our humanity. Perhaps we will finally listen to what she has been trying to tell us; I hope it's not too late. Meanwhile, my amygdala, the part of the brain that takes over when we are afraid, is blowing apart my rational self with its own hurricane-force winds.

I came to San Francisco as I have more than a dozen times before for inspiration, to re-engage with my "exploratory system," this time to start a new section of this book. I came to this city that lives inside my heart to rekindle my sense of adventure; but as I watch the news I don't feel adventurous at all. Why? Because like everyone else, my sense of adventure depends upon on how confident I feel in my secure base.

Watching the news reports of how different people were reacting to the coming storm, I started wondering about how their early attachment experiences were influencing them now. There is the surfer in his wet suit getting the most out of the beautiful waves that only a storm can provide a lover of extreme sports. Others are lingering on the boardwalks, knowing that the eventual mandatory evacuation will lead them to safety. The news also includes the sounds and sights of people boarding up their homes and businesses and stocking up on food and supplies. And then there are those being interviewed who are reporting with satisfaction that indeed they have already prepared an emergency stockpile, which is checked and replenished every few months as part of their normal routine.

During times of potential threat, we enter survival mode; and our brains are called to action to react and problem-solve. There is a growing amount of research indicating that one's ability to cope with stress and novelty is a result of our earliest life experiences with primary caregivers. These experiences create the individual brain-architecture that is used throughout our lives, including such once-in-a-lifetime experiences as

Hurricane Sandy. The reason why some of us will ride the surf while others prepare for the worst has a lot to do with the quality of our attachment with our earliest caregivers and how they helped us to regulate our earliest emotions.

Becoming attached is the most important mutual accomplishment of the infant and caregiver. The very quality of this earliest relationship will not only impact the child's emerging personality but will also shape the wiring of his growing brain.

To understand the importance of attachment, it is worthwhile to consider what the event of birth represents to an infant, what she gains and loses compared to life inside the womb. In the womb, the world is safe, dark and quiet; and everything she needs to live is provided for continually. Birth is a sudden and perhaps unwelcome world-change. From just one day ago, the world is now full of light and unintelligible noise. She must breathe, and experience the discomfort of hunger, excessive cold and heat, and a new world with people in it, whatever *they* are. The ability to become attached to a caregiver can then be seen as a blessing; it enables the baby to adapt to this thing we call life-after-birth. But while the baby is hard-wired to constantly elicit responses from its earliest caregivers, it is up to the caregiver to respond in an attuned way. Seemingly simple experiences such as being fed, held, and rocked become all-important to the infant, who is trying to regulate her feelings. As Lauren Lindsey-Porter summarized the process in *The Science Of Attachment*,

> In psycho-biological terms, babies are unable to regulate themselves. Despite being born with the capacity for feeling deep emotions, babies are unable to keep themselves in a state of equilibrium, lacking the skills to regulate either the intensity or the duration of those emotions. Without the assistance and monitoring of a caregiver, babies become overwhelmed by their emotional states, including those of fear, excitement and sadness.

This early bond provides the infant with his first secure base, the first foundation for the lifelong journey of emotional growth. From research in infant-attachment dating back to the 1950s, children can be described as being securely or insecurely attached, with securely-attached children more likely to explore the world out there.

These earliest infant-caregiver experiences enable the infant to decode and make sense out of their emotions. Over time they make up the baby's "internal working model" or template. From experiencing that his emotional world is understood, he learns not only to regulate his own emotions but also to understand the emotional world of others, in other words, to be empathic.

To the body of research in attachment theory that began after World War II has been added physiological research, which confirms the findings that are now over 50 years old and has upended again the traditional nature vs. nurture debate. Traditionally, it was believed that a person's genetic makeup is complete at birth. However, in the words of the neuropsychologist Dr. Allan Schore,

> There is more genetic material in the cerebral cortex at ten months, much more than at birth. What this means is that the genes are spinning out, programming well into the first year. They don't stop at birth. The genes that are encoding connections between parts of the brain that are coming on late, are in a very active state well into the first year. It is during this time that the potentiality of genes will either be realized or not.

Further, what realizes the potentiality of these genes is an "emotionally enriched environment that only humans can create." The benefits then of good infant-caregiver experiences are not only better emotional regulation but also better physical brain development. In Dr. Schore's definitive summary,

"Cells that fire together, wire together. Cells that do not, die together."

A Call to Action: Using What We Know

This knowledge about brain and personality development compels us to understand fully what enriches these infant-caregiver experiences and how we can provide them.

As part of my doctoral research in the late 1990s I visited and observed some of the best and most costly day-care programs in the New York area. Each of the programs provided inviting environments with age appropriate toys and supplies that promoted physical comfort; the atmosphere was friendly; and the teachers were happy. There was the usual contrast in the toddler rooms with some children playing quietly while others battled over coveted toys, the losers nursing their hurt feelings. The rapidly changing range of emotions included happy, sad, angry, and afraid as children displayed everything from uncontrollable giggling to face-to-rug meltdowns.

The caregivers did an extraordinary job juggling the children's needs for physical safety, human interaction, and the repeated, mirrored experience of their four basic emotions. It was amazing to watch each child try to get his needs met and learn about himself in the process as he tried to decode the meaning of each experience, sometimes with the help of an adult regulating his emotions, sometimes on his own. I also knew that each child brought to his toddler experience a self-view and a world-view that had been partly developed in the environment I visited next, the infant room.

Oh Baby!

In one infant room I was warmly greeted by a cheerful caregiver. She nestled an infant in her arms as she gave me the tour, checking on the other babies as they slept, gurgled or played in their crib. The room was fastidiously laid out. The changing stations were organized and clean; there was a place for sterilizing toys; and feeding and changing schedules were posted in plain view for the assistants. Looking at the schedules, I wondered aloud about the challenge of caring for all the babies uniformly. With a hesitant smile, my tour guide confided, "Sometimes I just pick them up if they're crying. I just can't leave them alone in their cribs." An assistant added, " You should have seen her this morning, a baby in each arm. She couldn't pick up Charlie who was having a fit. So I picked him up even though I am not supposed to. His parents left strict instructions."

Sensing my bemusement the assistant continued, "They don't want us to spoil him, otherwise they'll have to pick him up every time he cries at home. They want this experience to help him learn independence."

I found it sad that well-meaning parents did not understand that an independent child would not result from limiting the care given to their infant. These parents apparently also endorsed strict feeding and changing schedules as a promoter of cooperation and discipline. And so there it was, plain and simple, a state-of-the-art daycare center in the late 1990s still governed by conventional wisdom.

I hope that by now, as I write this, daycare policy has caught up not only with the current literature on attachment and brain development but also with the instincts of its own staff, which tells them to respond to the infants as much as possible and on demand, not on schedule.

The good news is that we now have enough evidence from the fields of psychology, child development, and neuroscience to demonstrate the vital role of caregivers — be they mothers, fathers or professional daycare workers —who dedicate their time to caring for infants. Right from the start, children use us to establish relationships that will help them regulate their stress levels. The attention they are seeking from us does not result in their becoming spoiled, rather it is essential to their human growth. As we help them make sense of their earliest feelings, they become securely emotionally attached to us. The attachment process is self-reinforcing: securely attached babies learn more effectively how to regulate their emotions and so feel less stress.

Bountiful Benefits

The information we now have helps us understand why the conventional wisdom contained in such expressions as "babies are exercising their lungs when they cry" and "manipulating us to get attention" is dangerously inaccurate. Attachment-chemistry studies, as summarized by Dr. William Sears, founder of Attachment Parenting, prove that consistent responsiveness in the earliest months creates the right balance of the stress-hormone cortisol. Where there is an imbalance of cortisol, both extremes are unhealthy; too little creates apathy whereas too much can lead to chronic anxiety.

This understanding and promotion of secure attachment has far reaching implications. According to Dr. Sears and his researchers, babies who do not need to use their energy to self-regulate will cry less and will spend much of that greater free time in a state of "quiet alertness." This alertness allows the baby to focus and be attentive to its environment; and when the caregiver responds to this quiet attentiveness, the baby is motivated to stay in this state even longer.

What emerges here from the research over the past 50 years in infant behavior and psychobiology is a positive growth-spiral which has infant-caregiver attachment at its core. When a caregiver responds to a baby's hardwired initiative to elicit care, the baby develops an internal working model based on a belief in secure attachment, which includes his first efforts at emotional self-regulation and empathy. This secure base also provides the infant with his first foundation to explore the world beyond.

All this happens in the first year of life. Now you can see why, without question, I consider becoming attached the most important mutual accomplishment of an infant and his caregiver.

Sharing Attention

Each day, the connection that an infant shares with a special person begins to set the stage for future attachments and for emotional and intellectual growth. In this period infants begin to develop their ability to pay attention. According to child psychiatrist Dr. Stanley Greenspan,

> In the first stage of emotional development, ordinarily in the first eight months of life, children are learning to attend and engage. This means simply the ability to share attention with another person. For a baby this would involve little Susie looking in her mother's eyes, focusing on her voice, or examining her mother's facial expressions. When shared attention is not developed, babies can become easily distracted or preoccupied.

Greenspan's elegant model describes four stages of development that occur in approximately the first four to five years of life: Engagement, Two Way Communication, Shared Meanings, and Emotional Thinking. It is his belief that mastering these stages enable children to "develop emotionally ... grow socially and cognitively as well" and that "ultimately the ability to think, that is to connect ideas and see relationships, is the result of this four-stage process that makes up the very foundation of learning." You will become very familiar with all four stages before the end of *The Mighty Milestones*. You are now familiar with the Engagement Stage, which occurs during the period of attachment.

First Lessons

The essential needs to idealize others and to be understood begin at birth. The caregiver's ability to respond empathically serves to calm the child as she learns about her place in the world: Is it safe here? Will my needs be met? Who can I rely on to help me make sense out of things as I learn about who I am? Can I trust the world? Is it safe to grow and to explore?

Becoming attached: a mighty milestone indeed!

Breaking Away

Like a seedling, a baby requires only the right kind of soil and nourishment. Then the energy of his growth processes will be able to do the job of pushing him into the world. The same growth processes ensure that the baby knows just how to reach out into the world and drink it in.

— Louise Kaplan

Adorable Ella strolls down Main Street with her mother and nana, the three generations celebrating the beginning of Ella's ninth month of life. It is a sunny spring morning, and all is right in her world. Ella is color-coordinated from head to toe, and looks quite fashionable with her hair pulled up into the tiniest ponytail atop her head. Mother and grandmother take turns pushing the stroller, accepting the occasional compliment from passers-by with gracious pride. Inside the stroller the little princess sits waiting to charm others with her flashy, toothless smile.

After a while Ella becomes more animated and wants out of the stroller. Her arms shoot up as her face beckons nana. Mom senses that they are on borrowed time and decides to stop for lunch. Inside their favorite child-friendly coffee shop, they begin the ritual of setting up Ella in a safety seat while mom rummages through her backpack for the travel toys.

There is a subtle change in Ella's mom as she patiently sets the stage for lunch. Her face grows more tense as Ella begins to hammer the table with her oversized plastic toy keys. As mom looks around to see who is annoyed by the banging, she isn't sure who is being bothered more: nana or the two businessmen at the next table.

"Ella, stop now sweetie. Nana doesn't like the noise." Indeed, nana's happy face has disappeared, replaced by a slight flush of embarrassment.

The businessmen look over with knowing smiles. "How old?" asks one.

"Nine months today," says the once again proud mother.

"She's a cutie," he adds. "I have a two-year-old at home. Just wait, that's when the trouble really starts."

This momentary break concluded, the men return to their negotiation.

Ella continues to wiggle in her seat playfully, dancing to music that only she can hear. Now it is time for the tossing game. Ella decides to toss her keys onto the floor and look at them until mom retrieves them, wipes them clean, and returns them to Ella's chubby baby hands. After Ella shakes the keys for a few more minutes she throws them onto the floor again; and after studying them for a minute, she gestures for mom to fetch them.

Feeling a bit foolish, mom picks up the keys to repeat the ritual.

Nana shakes her head, "You can't let her do that." And turning to her granddaughter she adds, "No Ella, you are being a bad girl now!"

Nana punctuates her discipline with a tiny slap to Ella's outstretched hand. Shocked by this sudden change in her world, Ella starts to cry. By reflex, mom puts the keys away and distracts her daughter with their recent favorite game, Peek-A-Boo. Within minutes Ella becomes again an adorable nine-month old responding to mom's playfulness while they wait for the food to arrive.

In my practice, I spend a great deal of time talking with parents about "separation/ individuation," a process that starts in the second half of the first year of life and lasts until early adulthood. That's how long it takes to experience oneself as fully independent, or fully *inter-dependent* to use the language of empathy.

And so the story of Ella is a common one. Three generations of women were in conflict because two of them lacked the knowledge to see Ella's behavior as a developmental accomplishment. Ella in the coffee shop was tackling the next mighty milestone: Breaking Away.

The Dance of Separation Begins

Ella had a blissful early merger with her mother during the first five months of life. It was just what she needed to understand the rhythm of her body, to maintain a comfortable equilibrium, and to get her emotional and physical needs met.

During this time an infant has an "illusion of oneness" with its primary caregiver; its body is an extension of the caregiver's and vice versa.

As the need for human attachment becomes satisfied, the exploratory urge of an infant such as Ella begins to develop. Louise Kaplan, in *Oneness & Separateness*, describes the first attempt at breaking away:

> The world is beckoning. The infant reaches his arms out to touch it. He stretches his body away from his mother. He perches at the edge of her lap. When she holds him, his leg and arm muscles push his body up so that he can be sure to have a good view of the world over her shoulder. His arms press against his mother's chest and his head inclines away from her face for a more distant perspective on her. The baby studies his mother's face with deep concentration as though he had never seen it before. The face he examines is not the face of the mother of oneness. The mother of separation is "out there" in the world — a mother in the flesh who lives outside the bounds of the baby's body, alongside the other things that are out there.

So, at five months Ella begins to see her mother as a separate person yet goes to great lengths to keep her close. She follows her voice and studies her movements. Other objects and people begin to fascinate her but never to the same extent. Everyone, especially her delighted mother, notices how her face grows brightest when sharing a mutual gaze. But Ella is faced with a paradox: how does she stay connected to her mother while attempting to explore her separateness? It begins to dawn on her that she will eventually need to be the master of her own body and her self.

Discovering Object Permanence

The developmental psychologist Dr. Jean Piaget taught us that children are not just small people; children, as part of their continual cognitive growth, make sense out of the world in an orderly way with their own special logic, which may appear "illogical" to adults.

Piaget defined various stages in the cognitive growth of a child, with each stage tending to occur around the same age in most children. Ella is in the "sensorimotor" stage, and as such she is beginning to see the world and its objects as something that are outside her body. When Ella's red ball rolls behind the playroom couch, she squeals in delight as she crawls around the couch to find it. Her discovery that toys or her mother still exist even though they are not part of her changes her world and her view of reality.

Imagine how exciting "object permanence" must be for a baby such as Ella. Her preoccupation with such classic games as Peek-A-Boo and tossing toys either from the high chair or out of the crib are attempts at exploring and solidifying this new cognition. Each episode of Ella tossing an object overboard, watching her mom retrieve it, and return it to her proves to Ella that the object still exists.

In the Peek-A-Boo game, where Ella's mom repeatedly covers and uncovers her own face, along with the exclamation, "I see you," she is satisfying Ella's normal developmental need to know that Mom always comes back after she disappears. Ella's mom is also helping her daughter begin to develop what Greenspan called "two way communication ... the ability to signal one's own needs and intentions." But in the coffee shop, nana was unfortunately trapped in conventional wisdom, worrying about her granddaughter being spoiled.

A Case of Object Constancy

The stakes were high for Katie's mom, a single working woman who needed the nursery school to keep her three-year-old daughter in the program so that Katie could get essential care and Mom could continue to work. Katie was having trouble sitting still for long periods and paying attention, especially during story time; and she had difficulty respecting class rules, such as staying out of the toy-closet after play. Overall, Katie required more attention and monitoring than the teachers could afford. I had been brought in by the director of the school; and it was agreed among the director, the mom, and myself that I would observe Katie in the classroom to try to understand why she was so unsettled.

Before beginning my close observation of Katie, I spent two days watching her from afar. I was introduced to the class as a "new friend" who was visiting, learning and playing. I sat cross-legged during story time, played puppets with the more curious kids, and created a beautiful finger-painting during art! Seeing that I was clearly having fun, by the end of the first day some of the kids were seeking me out for play; but Katie ignored me.

Keeping my distance, I noticed a difference between Katie's behavior and the others'. While she could participate in all the activities, she clearly had difficulty following directions and transitioning from one activity to the next; she wasn't interested in negotiating play with other children, and seemed unable to stay with class-projects to the end.

On the third day, I carefully shadowed Katie, playing alongside her but not looking at her. On the playground I ran around near her, mimicking her movements as she switched from ballerina to rock-kicker. When she went to the swings, I fitted myself most snugly into the seat next to her; and we pumped in unison and flew into the air. In one high-flying moment, I smiled at her and she smiled back.

When we returned to the classroom, I sat in the tiny chair next to her as each of us worked on our individual coloring project. I talked to myself as I composed my masterpiece, commenting on the colors I liked; but Katie was uninterested, tapping her feet as she scribbled large circles, inside her own world. At one point I noticed the blinking — blinking that every few minutes punctuated the rhythm of her coloring and foot-tapping. Suddenly she jumped out of her seat and ran into the book corner, dove into the bean bag, and closed her eyes.

While Katie was away, I asked the head teacher if she had noticed the blinking and what she thought about it. The teacher had observed Katie's blinking from time to time since the outset of school and wondered aloud to me whether it signified a tic disorder, which is often associated with ADHD.

I went back to my art work and waited for Katie. As suddenly as she had left, she flew back into her seat, sending the crayons and drawings from her desk onto the floor. She looked quizzically at these now distant objects and watched me as I slowly picked up each one and put it back where it had been before.

After a few minutes of quiet work, I told her how much I liked her picture. I pointed out how many circles she had drawn, how much she had used the colors green and yellow; and I asked her if they were her favorite colors. No answer. Instead she began to blink again.

"Katie is opening and closing her eyes," I said quietly. After a minute of silence, I repeated myself.

"Mommy." Katie looked straight into my eyes as she spoke her first word to me.

I replied to her directly, "You are opening and closing your eyes."

There was another moment of silence, and then Katie put it all together for us. "I see mommy," she said closing her eyes. Opening them, she looked straight at me, and then closed her eyes again, "I see mommy."

I Take You with Me

From my observations of Katie and my knowledge of her history, it was clear that her unsettled behavior was the result of not having a stable, internal image of her mother while she was managing her feelings at school. When she closed her eyes, Katie could conjure up an image of her mother; but she could not sustain it for very long.

Katie's mom had been able to care for her infant until her first birthday, and the two had formed a loving attachment. But then mom had to return to full-time work, leaving Katie with a different relative from one day to the next. Mom reported that her daughter would cry upon being left but could be distracted from her tears with a toy or her favorite snack. In relating this history, Mom's face revealed the pain and guilt that she felt from having to leave her daughter every day.

In time Katie seemed to adapt well to her new caregivers, with whom she became affectionate and compliant. Her mom proudly declared that her daughter had reached the developmental milestones of walking and talking on schedule, and she added that Katie's vocabulary was advanced for her age.

In response to my question about favorite pastimes, I learned that Katie loved playing run-away and hide-and-seek with her mom. She was also very much attached to her stuffed pooch, Corduroy, and wanted to take him everywhere including school.

Mom's greatest concern when I met her was Katie's fascination with the word "no" and her need to declare everything "mine." Her obstinacy often tested the patience of her devoted single mother, who after picking up her daughter each evening needed to complete the daily routine of shopping, feeding and bathing before putting her daughter to bed. Mom regretted being short with her daughter so frequently, and worried that it was getting harder and harder to keep her happy.

I could see that Katie was saving her most rebellious self for her mother. When I prompted Katie's mom on how she felt about that, with evident frustration she declared herself "a failure."

The case of Katie and her mom is not unusual. Conventional wisdom leads many parents to believe that they are doing something wrong when their children become so defiant. Katie was actually using her attachment figure, her mother, to work on an important developmental accomplishment: to prove to herself and the world that she had her own mind and her own self.

This milestone, object constancy, usually presents itself in the second year of life and is ushered in at a time when children, having learned to walk, become fascinated with exploring the world around them. It is with both excitement and fear that the toddler risks walking away from his caregiver to see "the world out there." Over and over again they practice, whether it is running down the hallway to another room or exploring the backside of the living room couch. With each adventure the toddler must have a sturdy sense of a separate self while believing that the accepting, supportive caregiver, the secure base, will be there to return to.

Adventure and the Secure Base

For Katie, the drama of breaking away was interrupted by having to accommodate herself to various caregivers each week. She had the impossible task of having to manage her need for adventure while staying connected to a secure base. Each day that Katie was left with a new caregiver she needed to put aside her exploratory needs so that she could create a temporary base in which she could feel safe. She would wait until her reunion with her mother to fully feel the ambivalence stirred up by her need to "grow up and away" while staying connected. Lesley Koplow, in *Unsmiling Faces*, summarizes how managing ambivalence is essential for a toddler achieving object constancy:

> He needs to counter the adult in order to feel his emerging autonomy. He needs to have the freedom to test the limits of the adult authority so that he can feel safe and contained as his own person within the secure boundaries provided by the adult. "No" helps him more clearly delineate himself from the other that he is opposing. "Mine" states his claim on the world and announces his intention to relinquish the passive infantile position for a more active, initiating role. By continually testing his parents and making sure that they are there when needed, the two-year-old is helping himself to internalize a constant parental presence.

Katie's reaching for independence was thwarted by both her Mom's inability to be with her during the day and the belief that her daughter's defiance of her was inappropriate. And so Mom and I created a program to simultaneously satisfy both of her daughter's needs: the need to experience being separate from her mother and the need to know that her mother was always there for her. Together, we created opportunities for Katie to experience what Dr. Margaret Mahler termed *rapprochement*, the child's need for a loving response upon returning to her mother after initiating a separation. For Katie, Mom would repeatedly play a version of hide-and-seek in which Katie would hide so that she could be found; and Katie would giggle in delight every time mom finished the game with

"Gotcha!" At bedtime, Margaret Wise Brown's classic tale *The Runaway Bunny* became a comforting ritual. Katie could imagine herself a wayward bunny whose mother would always bring her home. And when Mom read the lines, "If you run away, I will run after you. For you are my little bunny," she could feel proud of herself and joined with her precious child rather than rejected by her.

To help Katie feel her mother's presence in nursery school, Mom tucked photos of herself in the top flap of Katie's overalls, which she could pull out at any time. Even Corduroy played a role in helping Katie separate from her mother without feeling lost from her. Once it was understood that Corduroy was a "transitional object," something imbued with collected memories of being with Mommy, he was allowed to come to school for a time and "slept" in her cubby where she could always see him. According to Greenspan, these objects become "shared symbols" between parent and child, a prerequisite for sharing higher level information, and are also a way to bring Mommy along each day.

After a time Mom could see how her daughter's "bad behavior," the constant insistence of "no" and "mine," were actually part of a healthy attempt to gain power and independence. It was then that she could let go of the conventional wisdom telling her to extinguish her daughter's "early signs of defiance and selfishness," as she once had put it. Understanding her daughter's behaviors in a new way, she could respond with limit-setting that was not too harsh, knowing that she was doing a good job at parenting. For Katie's part, she could trust that she would not lose her mother's love and presence just because she was trying to be her own person. And so not only did Katie achieve the milestone of object constancy, she had her first successful encounter with tolerating ambivalence.

As Koplow summarizes,

> Over and over again, the toddler in his third year of life challenges himself to integrate the adult's shifting affects into one stable image. The mommy who says "no" is the same mommy who smiles a comforting smile and gives a bottle of milk. Once able to integrate positive and negative experiences with the nurturing adult, the child will have achieved object constancy: an ability to access the image of the nurturer even when he or she is out of sight.

As Katie and her mother did the needed "touch-up work," the troublesome behavior at school disappeared. Touch-up work, which I will discuss at greater length in *Kitchen-Table Therapy*, is work we all do throughout life, with those closest to us, to further some emotional growth not completed when the developmental opportunity first presented itself.

Autonomy

> Oneness is bliss. Separation is dangerous. And yet we pull and pull away. For the need to become a separate self is as urgent as the yearning to merge forever. And as long as we, not our mother, initiate parting, and as long as our mother remains reliably there, it seems possible to risk, even to revel in, standing alone.
>
> — Judith Viorst, *Necessary Losses*

> When the separation is stormy, it testifies to the strength of the ties which are being loosened.
>
> — T. Berry Brazelton

I was setting up for another Monday evening workshop, one in a series for my parent-support program at a local nursery school. Maybe it was the title "Disciplining Your Toddler"; for whatever reason, I was drawing in more people than I ever had. Seeing a lot of new faces, I scrambled for more chairs as my circle grew a second ring. I went around greeting parents and distributing handouts as everyone settled down; this sets an informal and inclusive tone, and gives me a feel for my audience. Amid the quiet chatter, I picked up one father's gruff sarcasm, "This should be good."

As I regularly did, I started off by going around the group, asking everyone what they hoped to get from the evening; and there was more frustration than usual in what I heard back. When it was his turn, Sir Sarcasm answered, "I just came because of her." The "her" turned out be his wife, who blushed and shot back, "Yes, and he really needs it."

I read my prepared remarks; and while everyone seemed to be listening patiently, I felt that I wasn't really being heard at all. As I finished talking about the origin of the word "discipline," I realized that I was not in anyone's experience except my own. Out of touch with the group, I quickly tacked to an interactive model so I could be more empathic. I went around the circle again, asking each parent to share what was hardest for them about discipline. As they continued to vent, I knew that I had found their language.

The common themes were feeling ineffective with and disrespected by their toddlers. One dad wondered how "such a little person could be so defiant and create such trouble." The group laughed when another exclaimed, "I feel like I'm walking a tornado on a leash." And one father volunteered, "When I was a kid, I would never have gotten away with what my wife lets him do."

I saw this last statement draw nods and sighs of recognition. This tipped me off. The first thing I had to do was to get these parents to talk about how they had been disciplined as children. Clearly their childhood experiences were shaping their parenting, and it wasn't working. What was widespread in this large group was parent fatigue syndrome.

I gave the group a needed break. When they came back (and I happily noticed that I hadn't lost anyone), I could feel the shift in mood. Everyone was more relaxed and open with each other; they were beginning to feel understood.

As a remembering exercise, I asked everyone to close their eyes and think back to their own childhood. Trusting me, they kept their eyes closed as I posed my questions.

"What memory do you have of the first time you said 'no' to your parents?"

"Do you remember where you were?"

"Who did you say 'no' to?"

"What did their face look like when you said 'no'?"

It was then that I saw the faces changing. There was grinning then grimacing; other faces seemed strained; and one woman looked to be on the edge of tears.

Gently I asked the group, "What happened after you said 'no'?"

I told everyone to take some deep breaths and open their eyes. With all eyes on me, I asked if anyone wanted to share what they had remembered. To my hidden delight, everyone wanted to share; no one wanted to be skipped.

In empathic unison, we all listened to each person's story, each summoning their own "ghosts in the nursery." Many of these parents, as children, were made to feel bad about saying "no"; others could not actually remember saying it aloud. Sir Sarcasm confessed that he wasn't allowed to say "no," and so he didn't until he was old enough to fight with his brother. For several, the word "no" brought a smack or a spanking; and they couldn't remember saying it to a parent again.

Saying Yes to the Word "No"

Allowing these parents to express what the word "no" meant to them became an essential part of the evening's workshop. It was only after they felt understood by me that they could take in information about their developing toddlers and their toddlers' needs for a certain kind of discipline as well as power.

As we in the group considered what the word "no" meant in the dictionary of conventional wisdom, we realized what we were up against. As the children of these parents were making the transition from infancy to toddlerhood, certain developmental accomplishments such as mobility, self-awareness, and language acquisition had changed the parenting landscape. The parents' need to set boundaries while accepting the "no" of willfulness had pushed them to a state of anxious ambivalence.

Dr. Jule Miller, in *Using Self Psychology In Child Psychotherapy*, speaks to the child's "will to do" as he describes emerging adversarial experiences:

> The parent's manner of handling the child's oppositional behavior, ambivalence and temper tantrums is very important for self development. With the change in the parent-child relationship there must be an adaptation on both sides. Although the earlier period of being a cute baby has passed, admiration must continue in some form for the child to develop normally. In spite of the stress that the willful toddler imposes on his parents, they must be able to take some pride in the strength of

his will. While they limit his behavior they must do it with compassion, realizing how frustrating these limits are to him ... if the limits are set with a sufficient admixture of empathy ... then the experience of running up against limits can leave the area of intolerable frustration and enter the realm of optimal frustration.

Walking, Talking, and Toileting

From this single evening's gathering grew a support group that stayed together for months and was in many ways the origin of the private practice I have today. Weekly the members came together to get information and to recall how their parents had responded to their "will to do" as children.

One evening, a frustrated young mother revealed, "Finally, I have the power. I never had it before, and it is hard to let it go." She expressed what many of the parents felt as they struggled to discipline their children. She was clearly frustrated, but resistant to changing her parenting that wasn't working. However, once she felt understood by the group, she was able to see how her unconscious memories of her early years had been influencing her ability to parent with joyful effectiveness.

In a very short period of time, these parents reported real changes at home, which of course was very gratifying to me. As a group, we had found the winning formula: to understand oneself better so that we as parents could understand our children's behavior in a new way. Previous "bad" behavior was now seen within the context of the child's attempt to grow.

I Can Walk Away from You

The typical toddler milestones, once a source of their parents' exasperation, were now a source of parental pride. We imagined what it was like to be a child who for the first time could stand up and actually launch himself into space, to take the first steps towards independence. And with that came the understanding of the child's profound ambivalence that must follow: the excitement of being able to move independently while being at the same time so dependent on the security of the caregiver. The parents came to respect "object constancy" as an essential need for managing this first ambivalence; children need to know that their parents exist and still approve of them even when they cannot see them. We shared with each other various ways we had created opportunities for the children to explore their environments while we waited for them at a safe distance.

The proud parents spoke less of the "terrible twos" and more of the "age of autonomy"; and walking a "tornado on a leash" became the group's signature phrase for describing what it takes to successfully manage toddler power. Most importantly, these once fatigued and frustrated parents understood that each child must find a way to practice, over and over, the need to be a separate person with her own ideas, and that the parent's role is to satisfy the idealizing need with safety, the mirroring need with admiration, and to accept the child's need to explore the world out there.

Words as Power-Tools

Emerging language became another important topic for the parents, who were now more naturally tuned into ways to help their children become more autonomous. Together we imagined how magical words must be to the child who first learns, "All I have to do is to say 'cookie' or 'Dada' and they appear!" We realized how idealizing it was for these children to know that attempts at communication could bring cooperation from their caregivers, who were also helping them to make sense out of their world. Everyone started to pay more attention to all language; even charming mispronunciations were taken more seriously. They understood that consistently responding to even primitive words and phrases reinforced what the children needed to know: putting ideas into words will make things happen.

As the children grew, so did the parents' understanding of what Greenspan described as "Shared Meanings," a developmental stage wherein children begin to use language "to relate their behaviors, sensations, and gestures to the world of ideas."

Further, they learned that when children say, "give me that," "I am happy," or "I am sad," they are using an idea, as evidenced in their words, to communicate something about what they feel, want, or are going to do. These are examples of Greenspan's concept of "Emotional Thinking."

It became easier and easier for the parents in the group to see the power of words; and words are the tools that all of us, adult and child, use to express our emotions without physically acting them out. We as parents all appreciated the importance of our nonjudgmental acceptance of our children's early attempts to express with words their four basic emotions — happy, sad, angry, and afraid.

With this understanding, we could laugh together as we did one evening to a father's imitating his daughter's exclamation, "Oh-wight, oh-wight, oh-wight," as she reluctantly got into bed. By being able to express herself in her way, she could obey without feeling powerless.

Everybody Poops

Exploring ways to help children feel autonomous continued as we discussed another major developmental accomplishment: using the toilet and saying good-bye to diapers.

Talking potty enabled me to share with the group one of my early discoveries as a mother: there are only three things that you cannot force a child to do — to eat, to sleep, and to toilet. I continued to explain, as they nodded in recognition, "You can't force a child to eat. If you do, they can spit it out. You can't make a child go to sleep unless they are drugged. And you cannot force a child to poop." And where a child has power is where there will likely be a parent-child power struggle. (And I believe that these power struggles can stay with us throughout our lives in the form of eating and sleep disorders as well as gastrointestinal problems.)

In our discussion of toileting, we realized that we were being held captive by the same conventional wisdom that had made the word "no" taboo. And this brought us back to the toileting experiences we had as children and whatever power struggles from that time had persisted into our adult lives.

One evening I shared a parenting book from 1907, written by a medical doctor at the College of Physicians and Surgeons at Columbia University, entitled *The Care and Feeding of Children: A Catechism for the Use of Mothers and Children's Nurses* by Dr. L. Emmett Holt. In this parenting group some 75 years later, we were shocked at what this esteemed professor was advising. Dr. Holt recommended that parents let babies "cry it out," that this was in fact "good ... essential daily exercise" for the lungs. He believed that a baby's flailing and stiffening was another opportunity for exercising the body. And regarding emotional interaction with the child, he instructed parents to refrain from too much affection with the child, and never to play with an infant under six months of age, lest they become "nervous and irritable."

His toileting method, which he believed should begin with infants at two months, seemed close to barbaric. He advised placing the infant on a chamber pot twice daily (at two months!), and at the outset stimulating the anus with "a small cone of oiled paper or piece of soap, as a suggestion of the purpose." His confident forecast was that "With most infants after a few weeks the bowels will move as soon as the infant is placed on the chamber."

Collectively, we realized how Dr. Holt's beliefs must have set up our parents for disappointment and failure; and we wondered what it took for them to reject the information of the time. We empathized with how confusing parenting must have been and acknowledged with pride how far they had come. After we reflected upon our parents and their toilet-teaching experiences with us, we were able to discuss with greater understanding how our children must feel about toileting. Widely held beliefs from the past were debated and put to rest as we began to see toileting as an early childhood experience of controlling one's own body, a wonderful opportunity for feelings of independence and autonomy.

In these final sessions of the support group, everyone was able to share the accomplishments of their children and themselves instead of the parent fatigue that had first brought us together. As the group said its good-byes, I realized that these parents were now meeting some of their own adversarial needs by confidently saying "no" to the conventional wisdom of the past. Just like their children, they were becoming more autonomous and powerful.

Parenting had become an opportunity for self- expression. These parents were now parenting artists, experiencing their own power daily. Unlike power through competition, the artist's power is not at the expense of others; rather it enriches the lives of others. And for this group the enrichment was of themselves and their families. For myself, I was a guide and first-hand witness to the constructive power of parental instinct: give a parent some good information and they will energetically do the rest. It is a formula I have repeated over and over again in my practice in the two decades since.

The Incredible Oedipal: Taking Initiative

And by giving up our passionate entanglement with our parents, we travel the oneness-to-separateness road yet again, moving into a world that can only be ours if we forsake our oedipal dreams.

Judith Viorst , *Necessary Losses*

From infancy, through toddlerhood and beyond, the growing child maintains his (or her) connection to his caregivers, upon whom he depends for survival, even as he begins to forge a separate identity. His parents, for their part, help the child grow up and away while keeping him close and connected. While navigating this emotional dilemma of individuation, the child also loses the innocent, enveloping warmth of early life. Lost are those times of being held close while being fed, the gentle caresses while being bathed, the loving, patient attention during diaper-changing, and the excited mirroring from Mommy and Daddy after first steps and first words. He loses, one by one, these most pleasurable experiences while being told that he is "too grown up" to need them anymore.

Among what is lost is access to the parental bedroom, the once warm and cozy snuggle haven. And does the child really get an explanation that makes sense to him? Most often, the justification for all these sacrifices is that he is a "big kid now," which may well seem a dubious status with an unclear payoff.

With feelings of anger, rejection, and separation-anxiety building up, the child undertakes a special initiative within the responsive family environment in which he feels safely nestled. Individuated, toilet-trained, and encouraged to be a grown-up, he imagines himself to be as powerful as his parent. And quite sensibly, he uses this fantasized power to regain what has been lost — at its core the original bliss with the caregiver.

This initiative by the child results in the oedipal struggle. With the help of the parents' artful negotiation, it is a stage in the child's emotional development, usually between 3 and 6 years of age, that helps him build a cohesive self while preparing for the future world out there. If this initiative is successful, the child can emerge from this period confident in his sense of power and his ability to achieve intimacy with another — his two infantile losses. And since the loving family is the whole world to the child, it naturally becomes the stage for his unique oedipal drama.

The Essential Triangle

"I really hate that kid sometimes!" exclaimed Dylan's mom.

She circled her eyes around my office, then reluctantly searched my face for the reaction she expected, the harsh judgment that would confirm her guilt.

"He is really making you angry," I replied softly. My empathic response brought fresh tears rolling down her swollen checks.

"Just talking about it makes me feel like a terrible mother."

As the session continued, she took one tissue, and then another, and another. Near the session's end she grabbed the last one out of the box.

"Did I break the record?" she asked, a smile breaking out over her strained face.

"You wonder if you have used the most tissues," I replied.

"I am all cried out. I used the most tissues because I am the worst kid-hating mom."

I responded, "I have learned that every parent hates their child at times. It is both necessary and normal. As they grow they need to push us away. They act hateful to achieve their goal. And they need us to stay constant and available. It is a real paradox."

"Maybe," she said wistfully. "Now you need to tell my husband that."

Dylan's mom and I spent the next session talking about what had motivated her to come for help. Their son, once the "love of their life," had recently become quite angry with his dad and only wanted to be attended to by his mother. The usual quiet of the house had been disrupted by endless door slamming and yelling. When I asked who was doing what, she replied, "Everybody."

It seemed that the once happy and affectionate boy could now only be satisfied with dear old Mom, and only some of the time. He repeatedly told his father to "go away," to "go live with nanny," and to sleep in the other room as the "bed was too small for the three of them."

Dylan's father was perplexed, to say the least; and he was taking it personally. His once adorable toddler was now cranky, dismissive, and uncooperative. At times Dylan would seek out his father to play "monsters and dinosaurs," usually when Dad was unavailable. Doing his best, he put aside time to play with his son, soon to find that Dylan thought the games were "too scary." Dylan would run out of the room crying, then return, his face red with anger. Sometimes he would call out for his mother. At other times he would give his father a punch on the leg before turning and running from the room. Mom would do her best to referee but felt exhausted in her failed attempts to bring the two together in the way it used to be. She had never seen her usually affable husband so short-tempered. It was really causing a rift in this young family's life. It was even suggested by a well-meaning relative that perhaps Dylan should be tested for ODD (Oppositional Defiance Disorder).

What I saw and described to my patient was that Dylan, at age four, had scripted an oedipal drama, casting both his parents in their appropriate roles. He was grasping for his mother's sole attention and seeking to expel his father from their triangle even though this triangle was his world and source of all caring. His parents' inability to respond appropriately to this oedipal initiative added to the ambivalence the oedipal child commonly feels when he (or she) fractures the domestic harmony which he is striving to regain, but which in its infant version is lost forever.

At the end of my explanation of Dylan's actions within the context of the oedipal phase of development, his mother sat back and chuckled, "Now I know what that was all about."

Then she paused, collecting herself to recall the elements of a clearly delightful memory.

Will You Be My Waffle-Headed Wife?

Dylan had recently accompanied his parents to a wedding — his first. Dressed like like a proper young gentleman in jacket and tie, he sat still through the entire ceremony, listening carefully to all that was being said. In the car ride home, both his parents told him how proud they were of his grown-up behavior. Dylan, alone in the backseat, thought quietly for a moment, gazing at the passing scenery. Then he turned towards his mother and asked, "Mom, will you be my waffle-headed wife?" Initially puzzled, both parents laughed when they realized their young son was imitating what he had heard in the chapel and that he was "popping the question." Sensing his feeling of ridicule, mom replied quickly, "Of course sweetie, you are the cutest."

In her telling, Dylan's mom conveyed her newfound awareness of how her remark could have contributed to the tension between son and father; she had unknowingly given her son an oedipal victory, something he really did not want.

The Birth of Desire

What Dylan really wanted was the validation of his initiative and the calm reassurance that his parents would not allow him to achieve his goal. In heterosexual families, the same-sex parent can help their child by telling him (or her) that they have "great taste," and by helping them imagine a time when they will have a wife (or husband) of their own. Such an empathic response helps cement in the young child's emerging self in important ways.

In accepting the oedipal defeat, the child breaks the triangle, and so takes a further step towards autonomy. The parents' role, through empathy and gentle boundary-setting, is to show the child that his thwarted ambition inside the family can be realized in the world beyond with their loving support.

It is also common for children of this age to identify with the parent that he (or she) seeks to displace once he realizes that he cannot get rid of his rival. This "if you can't beat 'em, join 'em" attitude can mark the beginning of father-son and mother-daughter activities (once again, in heterosexual families) which satisfy the child's idealizing and twinship needs, lowering the fear of parental retaliation while helping to build gender-identity.

Dylan, continually encouraged to be a "big boy," naturally used his parents' relationship to model and learn about grown up behavior. His growing cognitive ability also helped him to realize that they had something he wanted; loving feelings and actions that only they shared. His conclusion: "Dad must be the reason that I do not possess Mommy anymore."

What was Dylan to do? Because his thinking was still quite primitive, he imagined himself a powerful force, able to win back and merge with Mommy once again. The only problem, of course: the presence of Daddy! Dylan was now filled with a special kind of desire. This new wanting of something was also creating intensely ambivalent feelings toward his father. On one hand he loved and needed to look up to him while on the other he wanted to send him into exile. These competing feelings were both confusing Dylan and eliciting a fear of being retaliated against. His emotional conflict was especially evident in the play of "monsters and dinosaurs," where he could be strong and aggressive, only to run from the room worried and scared. Magical thinking was allowing him to see himself as all-powerful but was also encouraging fantasies of a larger, more powerful, and angry father.

Dylan's mother shared the information from our sessions with her frustrated and skeptical husband. With encouragement from his wife, he began to respond to his son in new ways. He found opportunities to to proudly tell his son how strong and assertive he was becoming, and father and son were able to resume their expressions of affection toward one another.

Over time, Dylan began to seek out his father even more for competitive game playing. And the father, who now saw these competitions as helping satisfy his son's adversarial needs, was able to participate more freely in his son's celebrations of age-suitable victories.

Dylan's parents used their wedding anniversary to revisit their son's "waffle-headed proposal." As they were getting dressed for their private celebration, Dylan barged into the bedroom and loudly asked, "Where are *you* going?"

Dad's tone was gentle and wise. "Hey buddy. I am taking my wife out to dinner. We have been married for eight years, this is a special night just for us."

Dylan plopped down on their bed, "No fair, I am married too."

"No Dylan, only I can be married to Mom. You will marry someone else someday."

Both parents held their breath in anticipation. Dylan jumped up and down on the bed a few times, and then paused in a characteristic moment of reflection.

"Daddy, can I use your Ipad when you're out?" he asked as his parents exhaled with great relief.

The Wisdom of Dr. Freud

Sigmund Freud provided the original psychoanalytic explanation of the oedipal phase, whose unhealthy resolution would lead to an "oedipal complex."

My approach to handling the oedipal phase is based on what I have learned from Self Psychology and what its founder, Heinz Kohut, believed about this period. In *How Does Analysis Cure*, he states,

> The healthy child of healthy parents enters the oedipal phase joyfully. The joy that he experiences is due not only to the fact that he himself responds with pride to a developmental achievement, that is to a new and expanding capacity for affection and assertiveness, but also to the fact that this achievement elicits a glow of empathic joy and pride from the side of the oedipal phase self-objects [i.e., parents].

For me, the framework of Self Psychology focuses on the positive, growth-enhancing aspects of this important period, in contrast to the classical Freudian focus on the complex, a conflicted emotional state full of fear and guilt, that results from un-empathic parental responses. This expanded understanding of the oedipal phase makes it more palatable for parents who may have been turned off by Freud's original proclamations. For some parents, his theory seems outlandish; and so they discount it entirely, leaving them uninformed and unprepared for this important milestone.

Freud believed that oedipal children are working through intense feelings of sexual attraction for and a need to possess the parent of the opposite sex. However, an updated understanding of early sexuality as it relates to parents and children provides less support for Freud's argument. As expressed by Dr. Richard Gardner in *Understanding Children: A Parent's Guide To Child Rearing,* "I believe that there is a biological sexual instinct that attracts every human being to the opposite sex. ... From birth to puberty this drive is not particularly strong because during this period the child is not capable of fulfilling the drive's primary purpose of procreation."

All psychoanalysts, including this author, are indebted to Sigmund Freud. His brilliant and courageous work in the late 19th and early 20th centuries remains the foundation for the practice of therapists such as myself a century later. The modern-day differences with Freud represent a refinement of his theories, not their repudiation. At the time of this writing, heterosexual families still dominate the research and understanding of how children develop. As our culture shifts to accommodate new family constellations, there will be further refinements in our understanding of how children use this phase in an expansive and joyful way. The oedipal drama requires a triangle so that the child has an opportunity for assertiveness and desire. I believe it is the experience of the triangle, not who is in the triangle, that is needed for growth in this developmental phase.

As we continue to understand the importance of parental responsiveness during this stage, we must address what happens when a triangle is nowhere to be found.

"Now Kiss!"

Five-and-a-half-year-old Jennie sat at the top of the stairs, listening to her parents arguing below. Wanting to wear her "silky pants" to school, she was annoyed that she could not get anyone to tell her where they had disappeared to. It was just another morning of having to wait until her parents voices grew silent so that she could insert her own.

"Well, that's just great," she heard her dad say in his rumbling voice.

"I told you about this a month ago," her mother shot back.

"Oh yeah? Where was I?"

Jennie knew Dad was really mad, but she just wanted her silky pants. The front door slams, and Dad is off to work again without saying good-bye. Silence, finally.

"Mom, where are my silky pants?" Jennie calls out from upstairs.

Silence. Jennie takes it up a notch, kicking the wall at the top of the stairs.

"Mom I want my silky pants, I can't find them."

"Jen, wear something else. They are going in the wash," Mom finally responds.

"No, I want my silky pants!" she cries furiously.

Jennie's mother climbs the stairs. Fatigued and defeated, she retrieves the pants from the hamper and hands them over. "Please. Now get dressed for school."

Trophy in hand, Jennie complies. The life of a child with parents going through a rough patch.

At the dinner table that evening Jennie excitedly recounted her day at school.

Dad, sitting on one side of her responded warmly, "That's great honey."

Her mother murmured in agreement.

Jennie eyed one parent, then the other, and finished her dinner in silence.

After dinner the three settled into the nightly ritual of television in the den, Jennie in the center. At one point she jumped up to bring her bemused parents next to one another other.

As if they were stubborn furniture she pulled and pushed, grunting in her determination to get Mom and Dad side by side. Her labor completed, she stood in front of them and commanded, "Now Kiss!"

The Case of the Missing Triangle

In our sessions, Jennie's mother and I had been talking about her marriage for some time. She and her husband had grown far apart, and it had been quite some time since they had shared any intimacy. Both had reached the stage in their professional careers where they were constantly in demand; as a result, it was common for one parent to arrive home just as the other was leaving. They were doing their very best to be there for their child and couldn't understand why, amid their loving sacrifices for her happiness, Jennie had become so stubborn and hard to please. A recent, last-ditch effort at marriage counseling was failing; and the couple was discussing divorce.

I could see that in such an inharmonious marriage Jennie wasn't getting from her parents what she needed most in order to work on her oedipal milestone: a romantically involved Mom and Dad. The initial reaction of Jennie's mom to my explanation reflected her emotional defeat, "This is the one thing I don't think we can give her."

Through my work with the mom, however, both parents came to understand the implications of preparing for divorce while their daughter was working through her oedipal stage: Jennie was presented with the all-too-real possibility that her fantasied ambition to defeat Mom and keep Dad all to herself might succeed. As a result, Jennie's natural efforts to script a rift between the parents left her feeling unnaturally afraid.

Jennie's parents accepted the responsibility of getting divorced while a child was immersed in the oedipal struggle. They worked together to minimize their anger and fighting during the separation, to reassure Jennie repeatedly that she had never had done anything to cause the divorce, and that there was nothing she would ever do that would lead either of them to "divorce" her.

It was a difficult time. But Jennie and her mom found a bond in watching the classic romantic movies together. Seeing Mom's interest in the on-screen adult romances, Jennie could envision such a romance for herself. Often after a movie, the young girl would talk to her mother about the kind of man she would marry when she grew up. Mom's encouragement of Jennie's ambition to find her own adult romantic partner helped this oedipal girl to identify with her mom, and to see her as supporting such an initiative without fear of retaliation or competition. In this way she began to to resolve her oedipal struggle within the limits of what can be achieved when parents are divorcing.

Taking Initiative: The French Toast Rebellion

At age six, Cole had a favorite meal; it was french toast for breakfast. It was a treat since it only happened on a weekend when his working parents had enough time for the preparation. Almost like a celebration, it began while he was still in bed, being awakened by the sounds and smells rising up from the kitchen. Added to Cole's excitement was the opportunity to please his mother, a newfound ambition.

Wide awake, he waited for his mother's sweet voice to beckon him downstairs with the familiar expression, "Hey my little man. Time for breakfast."

As he was racing downstairs, he caught himself and ran into the bathroom to wash his face. She loved it when he remembered to do that.

Recently, his enjoyment of the ritual had shifted from the flavors of butter and syrup to the demonstration of his grownup domestic skills, which he noted that his two-year-old sister, Lillie, did not possess. He especially loved clearing the dishes at the end of the meal, and bringing them over to his mother at the sink, seeing the loving expression on her face, and hearing her tell him how he was her "favorite helper."

Cole's father was busy with Lillie as he entered the kitchen that morning. He knew that his sister had been giving his parents a hard time of late, something about "the terrible two's." He didn't really know what that meant, only that Lillie was getting yelled at a lot; but he did enjoy being told that he was "such a good boy."

Lillie's face lit up when she saw her brother, immediately telling her father that she wanted "down" from her booster seat.

"Me play Cole, me play Cole," she insisted with her small collection of words. She countered her father's impatient request to sit still with a quick "no!" her face now wrinkled with anger.

Bringing the french toast over to the table, Mom nervously asked her son to help out by sitting down next to his sister. He did so quickly, feeling the gratitude of his mother's soft kiss on his very clean forehead.

With everyone seated, it seemed that they could finally enjoy breakfast; but Lillie had other ideas. As Dad cut her toast into toddler bites, she started to squirm in her seat; and the father-daughter battle was rejoined.

"Lillie, stop," he said angrily.

"No, play Cole now."

"Take a bite for mommy," he cajoled.

"No!"

"Okay, then take a bite for Cole," he patiently offered.

It seemed like Dad had finally found the right words. Lillie studied her prepared plate and reached for some french toast with her new Gerber baby fork. Looking at her brother she held up some food and then with a ceremonious smile flung it onto the floor.

"That's it Lillie!" yelled her father, his patience snapped. "Fine, now you will have no french toast. Did everyone hear that? No french toast for Lillie. No eating for Lillie today. I am throwing it all away."

Even before his father finished, Cole stood up and slipped behind his baby sister. Pressing his nose to her small head he offered her a piece from his plate and said soothingly, "It's ok, Lillie. It's ok. No one will take away your french toast."

Cole sat back down triumphantly glaring at his father.

"Tom, is this necessary?" his wife asked, trying to broker a peace.

"Enough. I have had enough. And Cole, you go to your room, now!" Tom shouted.

"No, I won't," replied Cole, sensing victory.

"Oh yes you will. Now."

Cole began to cry, "No fair, I want breakfast."

"Breakfast is over," Dad declared.

"Please do as your father asks," Mom quietly pleaded to her son. "Please Cole, do it for me. I will save you some french toast for later."

Because she had asked, Cole left the kitchen with a defiant kick to his chair.

Revisiting the Ghosts

Tom, Cole's father, sighed as he retold this oedipal tale in my office. He was sure that he had really "messed up" at the breakfast table, which added to his worry that he was "losing it" with the kids and losing his wife's support as well.

He was a devoted father, and the recent chill to the warm family circle had left him feeling lost and alone. He was resentful towards his own son who had become distant and antagonistic and not just at the breakfast table. And even his precious Lillie, taking her first steps at individuation, was driving him crazy. Completing his isolation was his wife's alliance with the children. She seemed to be constantly "doting on the kids" with endless amounts of concern for their feelings. All of this left him feeling like a callous ogre.

Tom thanked me for letting him "rant" as he put it. His venting, as I would put it, was important for him not only to express his deep and genuine sentiment for his wife and children, but also to reconnect with that sentiment and so to regain his self-image as a devoted husband and father.

Feeling understood, Tom began to revisit his own childhood memories of the relationship with his father, a bully who was impossible to please. His mother, a weak and ineffective woman, relied heavily on her son for support especially when he grew into a strong adolescent boy. Tom could not remember any good times with Dad, only that his mother needed him to protect her. He recounted one episode sadly, recalling the alarming and fearful process of phoning 911 one evening and waiting for the police to arrive — all to keep the family safe. Now a father himself, Tom still remembered how afraid he had been of "really wanting to hurt" his dad.

Tom's own oedipal strivings had been severely damaged by the circumstances of his life. He never got the chance to compete with his father in a healthy way but was instead left with unresolved worries that no good could ever come from being angry; as a result, he never got from his father what he now needed to give to Cole: a non-aggressive acceptance of his young son's need for autonomy and strength. Instead, his son's normal attempt at an oedipal accomplishment was triggering unconscious memories, the ghosts of parents past.

Over time Tom's new awareness helped him to respond to his son differently. He created appropriate opportunities for his son to compete with him and responded more patiently to Cole's continuing attempts to make things right with Lillie. Tom realized that Cole was competing with him in areas that were more properly a father's domain, such as disciplining Lillie. He and his wife together guided Cole back to being a six-year-old son, not a surrogate father or husband. Tom told Cole how proud he was of his stepping up to Lillie's defense, how lucky she was to have a protective older brother, but that it wasn't good for his sister to keep her wild ways at the breakfast table.

Cole's mom stopped calling her son her "little man" as both parents understood that this phrase could be making him feel as if he was somehow replacing his father.

Cole soon got the message that he did not need to protect either his mother or baby sister and that his father was patiently in charge.

Grand Assertions

Cole's healthy oedipal resolution became evident in an episode of their nightly bed-time authority-competition. Cole was negotiating to stay up later while seeking to keep the routine of Dad's tuck-in.

"Dad, can I stay up until I fall asleep?"

"OK son, that's fine," Dad says while kissing his son goodnight.

"Dad, when I grow up, can I be a great lawyer like you?"

"Sure, son. I bet that you can be an even better lawyer than me."

More books to read!

Touchpoints: Your Child's Emotional and Behavioral Development, by T. Berry Brazelton, M.D.

The Magic Years : Understanding & Handling the Problems of Early Childhood, by Selma Fraiberg.

Playground Politics: Understanding the Emotional Life of Your School-Age Child, by Stanley Greenspan, M.D.

Oneness and Separateness: From Infant To Individual, by Louise Kaplan, Ph.D.

Dairy of a Baby, by Daniel Stern, M.D.

Part Five

The World Beyond: School Daze

The ideal school should serve as a mediator between home and the wide world of reality, and should be a place not merely for book knowledge, but a place in which the knowledge and art of living should be taught.

— Alfred Adler

My daughter is grown now, but I still remember her elementary school and what wonderful years they were for both of us. For me, it was a chance to watch my precious child launch herself into the world. For her, it was an opportunity for innate talents to emerge as she navigated her way through new experiences, curriculum, friendships, and being away from home.

One particular memory captures all that I treasure from that time. I had come to her school to pick her up early. Seated in the lobby, I looked down the long hallway that led to her classroom. I knew that I would see her at any minute; the school secretary, who made it her business to know everyone, had alerted the teacher to my arrival.

Breaking the quiet, the door opened; and out she flew, arms juggling all her school paraphernalia, including her latest, not quite dry yet, art masterpiece. Seeing me, her steps quickened. As she approached, her face held such an expression of joy that I found my spirits being buoyed as well.

Alive with excitement, she dropped everything to give me hug.

"Well, someone is really happy to see her mom," observed the secretary, taking it all in.

"Yes. *My* mom is here at *my* school," my first grader boasted.

Looking back, I realize that this mirroring moment gave both my daughter and me just what we needed: someone we knew and trusted who saw our connection and spoke of it out loud. Empathic responses such as this from caring educators are what empowered my daughter to bridge the gaps between school, home, and the world beyond.

Taking the Show on the Road

To reach a child's mind a teacher must capture his heart. Only if a child feels right can he think right.

— Haim Ginott

Our children enter school with a profound need to use the environment to further learn who they are and to cement in the developmental gains achieved at home. They will need many experiences where they feel accurately understood and opportunities where early grandiosity can be expressed. Naturally they will have many frustrations as they learn about themselves and others; these frustrations need to be optimal to help them develop tolerance for ambivalence and disappointment.

As parents prepare to send their children to school for the first time, they have a right to know, among other things, how their children's essential needs will continue to be provided for. My purpose in this section is to cite examples from my practice where the problems facing parents of children in school were due to the essential needs being ignored and how the teacher's shifting his or her focus toward these needs allowed the child to blossom.

From Stupid to Stupendous

Robin described herself as a learning-challenged child who spent her early school days feeling compromised and stupid. She grew up in the 1950s, a time when we knew very little about learning differences as defined by Howard Gardner and Thomas Armstrong. Even her parents had come to accept that while she had a lovely disposition she was "slow." By the time Robin reached the sixth grade, school had become an unhappy chore.

Then she met the beloved, crazy Mr. B, her Social Studies teacher, who taught unconventionally even by today's standards. He didn't lecture from the blackboard; he didn't ask that everyone sit quietly in rows; he used films as much as textbooks. He would continually move among the students, selecting some of them to read out loud from the text, then create mini-plays where they could act out what they had learned or let them draw and build models that represented key concepts. And with an eye for those sixth-graders who were natural teachers, he asked a couple of students to provide extra help to others who were working more slowly.

Mr. B's social studies class was as far from the "worksheet wasteland," as Thomas Armstrong called it, as a classroom experience could be. By the middle of the year, the whole classroom was filled with talented students eager to show off what they knew. In such a community of collaborative learners, no student was left behind.

Even in the semester's final exam, an experience of special dread for Robin, Mr. B showed his great skill. While traditional in its design, it did not try to confuse or trick the students from choosing the right answer. Rather he wrote it so that each individual student could demonstrate all that he or she had learned.

Robin had been well-schooled in humiliation; so on the day when the tests were to be handed back, she braced herself. She sat numbly at her desk as Mr. B walked slowly around the room, speaking briefly to each student as he returned their paper. Then he approached her, placed the test on her desk, and said, "Robin, this is really stup- ..."

In her mind, she heard the word "stupid." What else should she expect?

"Robin, this is really stupendous! Well done," he said and moved on to the boy next to her.

Hearing from a teacher that she was stupendous, not stupid, marked a turning point in her life. Decades later, now a teacher herself, she holds this memory close as she brilliantly works with learning-challenged children.

Teachers as Idealizing Figures

In the classroom, Mr. B provided Robin with the essential experience of idealization. While always keeping control of the class, he found creative ways to help his students feel powerful. As a result Robin never felt as calm elsewhere as she did in his highly energized environment. Her poignant memories of her beloved Mr. B underscore just how important teachers are in the world beyond home.

As one of my idealizing figures, psychologist Haim Ginott, wrote during his years as a teacher,

> I have come to a frightening conclusion. I am the decisive element in the classroom. It is my personal approach that creates the climate. It is my daily mood that makes the weather. As a teacher I possess tremendous power to make a child's life miserable or joyous. I can be a tool of torture or an instrument

of inspiration. I can humiliate or humor, hurt or heal. In all situations it is my response that decides whether a crisis will be escalated or de-escalated, and a child humanized or de-humanized.

Teachers as Mirrors

Off to school our children go every morning ready and eager to receive a positive reflection back from the world out there. Poet Kahlil Gibran wrote, "Show me your mother's face, and I will tell you who you are." School-age children have a similar experience with their teacher: Show me my teacher's face, and I will tell you how I feel about my ability and talent.

My young patient Jason was a child with a lot of "kinesthetic intelligence"; he learned best when he could move around as well as touch and manipulate objects. He thrived in pre-school and kindergarten; but when he entered the first grade and had to follow the rules of the traditional classroom, such as sitting still, he became a "discipline problem." Accustomed to the former good rapport with his pre-school teachers, this once spirited child became torn between wanting to "be a good boy at school" and his absolute need to use his body to learn. By the late autumn of his first grade year, he was showing signs of depression in and out of the classroom; he had lost his once rampant enthusiasm and seemed more tired than usual. So his parents sought me out.

Fortunately, Jason's elementary school was quite receptive to working with his parents and me. Once we understood the dilemma, his dedicated teacher took in everything I shared about Howard Gardner's theory of multiple intelligences and how they relate to learning styles. She quickly created additional class curriculum which allowed him to use more of his natural talents instead of having to suppress them. He was allowed to scribble in a spare notebook, which helped him to sit still and listen. Taking advantage of the sign language skills he had learned from his mother, an ASL teacher, she helped him teach the other children to sign; and together the children used sign-language to create letters, words and concepts in the classroom. The more that Jason could move while he learned, the more grand he felt; and because his abilities were now more prized, he was able to sit still longer during times when it was absolutely necessary.

Most importantly, his parents, teacher and I got Jason back onto the track of healthy development. He no longer had to hide his talents in order to be at school. And he could better tolerate his frustrations as he came to trust that there would be parts of the school day that would allow his talents to emerge and his ambitions to be recognized.

The teacher discovered other multiple intelligences among the children in her class; and by adapting her curriculum accordingly, she happily reported an overall increase in classroom cooperation.

Teachers Understanding Twinship

During my tenure at a local university, I taught child development to teachers enrolled in a Master's Program in School Counseling. The curriculum covered much of the material in this book. The following vignette was told to me and others in my class by one such teacher-student, Gail, whose evolving understanding of children's emotional needs helped her repair the distorted twinship needs of one of her third graders.

Ruby was having trouble socializing both in and out of the classroom. Gail described her student as somewhat of a free-spirit, someone who always had something unique to add to classroom discussions albeit with a haughty tone, as if she knew better than her fellow third-graders. Gail sensed that this attitude was not inviting friendship into Ruby's life.

One day, Gail arranged the students into small groups so that they could work together on a class project. As she walked around the room checking in to see how they were doing, she overheard Ruby saying, "I am *not* bossy!" This brought the response from a classmate, "Oh yes you are Ruby, *everyone* thinks so." Gail saw Ruby's expression change from superiority to pain; the rebuke had stung.

To better understand Ruby's need for haughtiness, Gail arranged a one-to-one meeting over lunch. One lunch turned into several, resulting in precious time for both student and teacher. Ruby shared stories about her family, especially her mom, a clothing designer with a signature style. Her mom really hated doing things the way everyone else did; her favorite expression was, "I am an original." She would have talks with her daughter about this, especially when clothes shopping, constantly reminding her that doing things like other people was "just not cool." With her insistence that Ruby be totally unique, she was unknowingly denying her an important developmental step: an emerging need for twinship experiences.

Gail, with the knowledge of child development and empathic skills gained from her coursework, used the next parent-teacher meeting to explain the importance of twinship to this mother who placed such a priority on uniqueness. She helped her understand that it was essential for a girl of Ruby's age to feel *just like* some others in her class, otherwise children can feel like weirdos or alone in the world. This mother was surprised and reassured to learn that it is when children can feel an alikeness with others, they feel safe enough to show off what makes them different.

From that point, Mom relented and allowed her daughter to wear some of the latest "fads," and agreed to follow the crowd to the ice-cream cafe favored by everyone after school concerts.

Gail shared her triumph in my class one evening, reading out loud from Ruby's *Who I Am* essay, where the third-grader declared, "I am not bossy. I have such good ideas. Sometimes I feel like a dress worn inside out. I want to fit in, not out."

With these words Ruby acknowledged her need for continued twinship experiences, to which her teacher and mother now knew how to respond.

Teachers Supporting Adversarial Needs

The healthy fulfillment of adversarial needs, as Self Psychology defines them, requires special explanation. Such needs, which crop up commonly in sibling rivalry, have a better chance of being met appropriately inside a loving family environment than in the world beyond. Nevertheless even inside the family circle, the conventional wisdom surrounding winning vs. losing obscures the proper understanding of adversarial exchanges, leading to a greater risk of the distorted satisfaction of such needs.

Through the healthy use of adversarial exchanges, we meet the essential need to see ourselves as distinct individuals, separate from others. While this definition puts adversarial needs opposite twinship, the two Self Psychological needs co-exist. We are all similar to other people and different from them at the same time; after all, without any differences we might lose our sense of self.

A key to the healthy satisfaction of adversarial needs is to accept being a different person without being better or worse than another. I hope that everyone reading this book sees this distinction; but it might not be so easy for our children, who seek to make sense of a world dominated by zero-sum competitiveness. As they try to get their absolutely essential adversarial needs met in the classroom and beyond, they will need repeated exercises and constant monitoring.

In school, the prevalence of involuntary win-lose competition leads to the unhealthy, distorted satisfaction of adversarial needs. As parents we cannot erase the conventional wisdom around the virtues of competition, but we can work to provide our children with healthy opportunities for getting these needs met both at home and in the classroom and to insist that our children's teachers are equipped to do the same. As teacher-educator Rick LaVoie (F.A.T. City) explains,

> One of the practices we use in school to motivate kids is competition. The idea is to have kids compete against each other in order to be more motivated, and we have been using it for years, and it simply does not work. Eighty-five percent of what we do in the elementary and middle-school classroom is competitive in nature. And we do that because we believe it is motivating and its getting them ready for the big bad world, and neither of these things are true. The most important thing to understand is that the only person motivated by competition is a person who thinks there is a chance of winning. The competition we use in school is nothing like the competition in the real world. The competition in the adult world meets two criteria. ... In adult competition you only compete when you want to, and when we compete, we only compete against peers. I don't want anyone saying that I said that kids shouldn't compete. No. Should kids play high school football? You bet. Any competition where a kid can have input whether or not he competes and when he competes against peers, I'm okay with that. But if eighty-five percent of what we do in the classroom is competitive in nature, you are not going to convince me that even a fraction of that meets the criteria of adult competition.

Crippling Competition

Alana's parents came for a consultation because their fifth-grade daughter was getting into trouble at school. Linguistically gifted, as she would be described in Howard Gardner's *Frames of Mind*, she seemed intent on using her words to create conflict. She considered the classroom rules annoying and quickly lost her temper when her teacher tried to correct her behavior, always blaming others for her shortcomings. Her excessively argumentative style was alienating her classmates as well as her teacher, who could barely get through the day without an Alana-incident. Her behavior pattern was leading her teacher and the school psychologist to be jointly concerned that she could be suffering from Oppositional Defiance Disorder.

Her parents reported tremendous sibling rivalry among Alana, their middle child, and her two brothers. Even though the parents went to great lengths to treat all three children equally and fairly, they could not get rid of the constant rivalry, with each child measuring his or her success against the failure of another. Since Alana was more verbally advanced than her brothers, that was the skill she used to compete with them.

The parents came to understand that the sibling rivalry was causing exaggerated adversarial exchanges in the classroom. It was not enough that Alana's opinions were different from others', they had to be better than others'. And as happens with deeply engendered rivalries, the child's reinforcement from winning more than offsets the fear of the adult's anger over the bickering; so the cycle continues.

The competitive emphasis of the school curriculum filled Alana's day with opportunities to do what she did at home to gain approval: win at all costs. Each time she won the spelling bee or got the highest grade she felt superior to the others. All she understood was that the success of her ideas was based on the failure of others'.

Meeting with Alana's teacher gave us the opportunity to share information so that she could find ways to help all her students "do their personal best rather than striving to be the best," as LaVoie coined the idea. She began by placing less emphasis on grades in her classroom and kept them more private than she had before. She also stopped posting good and bad behavior on the blackboard and instead met privately with the students to help them understand appropriate classroom protocol.

Alana's teacher was quite pleased with herself as the classroom atmosphere became less competitive. She especially loved implementing several activities that I suggested in order to help promote healthy adversarial exchanges among all her students. Her favorite, "The Public Statement," was just one of many that can be found in *100 Ways To Enhance Self-Concept In The Classroom*, by Canfield and Wells.

This exercise is designed to help children voice their opinions in a non-judgmental environment; they are allowed five minutes to say something to which the classmates and teacher will listen without rebuttal. All the students grew to love their "five minutes of fame," a time to control the eyes and ears in the room, even the teacher's. Although no debate was allowed after these statements, the children were invited to write opinion papers in reaction to what they had heard. And while these papers were collected and read by their teacher, they were never graded. Similar exercises were implemented throughout the school year, each of them promoting self-awareness as well as a tolerance for differing viewpoints. There were no right or wrong statements made during these precious times, just the opportunity to be oneself without losing the support of others.

At home, Alana's parents began to treat each child differently and equally. As each sibling developed more of their own identity, the household rivalry began to diminish.

The parents' sense of achievement was capped one evening at the dinner table when Alana announced that she was helping her teacher start the very first "Diversity Club" at her middle school.

Reforming Education Reform

As I write this book, in 2013, the United States is in the middle of an anxious re-evaluation of its educational system. I am optimistic that we as a nation will bring our system up to its potential; but the recent news on education has made parents less sure about what to expect, yet another contributor to parent fatigue.

This year marks the 30th anniversary of President Reagan's school reform initiative, *A Nation At Risk*. Reflecting on this initiative, Deborah Kenney, CEO of Harlem Academies and author of *Born To Rise*, concludes that after 30 years the U.S. is now "a nation in crisis." Expanding on this comment and the subject of education reform, Dr. Kenny observes,

We are now in an economy that is completely based on education, it is a knowledge economy. The future of the country, national security and the economy, not to mention the moral fiber of the nation, are all based on education ... The public is more aware that the education system is failing, and people are demanding accountability. Common core standards have brought the country together. Actually, I have a concern about the direction of education reform itself. I think the education reform is based on a paradigm of controlling teachers, you know, reward and punishment and evaluation ... controlling teachers through policy. You can't be evaluating every individual person from a government system. Lots of our states and cities are spending tens of millions of dollars creating curriculum. We have curriculum, we need to develop people. We have to create a culture that brings out passion. You have to give people more freedom and autonomy. The teaching profession needs to be elevated ... we need a more powerful vision for what we are looking for ... what kinds of education are we looking for?

The Politics of Conventional Education Reform

As we struggle to figure out how to educate our young citizens, I believe some core principles are being neglected. Policymakers talk about raising test scores as if they are the only measure of academic success. And in addition to the great pressure being placed on students to perform, teachers are now worried about the need to meet "the new tougher standards" and the demands of "teaching to the test." I cannot fathom how such education reformers, who must know that fear shuts down the brain's ability to learn, expect higher academic performance to follow from higher classroom anxiety.

What education reform largely misses is that the curriculum being developed is doing little to help both teachers and students have the absolutely essential experiences needed for intellectual and emotional growth. As demonstrated above, I believe it is teachers who provide these experiences and that parents must support those teachers who do so.

Education Reform: Starting Early

The human infant is amazingly capable of compliance. He can be shaped to walk at nine months, recite numbers at two, read by three, and he can even learn to cope with the pressures that lie behind these expectations. But children in our culture need someone who will cry out, "At what price?"

— T. Berry Brazelton

The continuing necessity of two-income families and the legislative initiatives for public pre-K increase the importance of excellent early childcare programs that provide the essential experiences children get from primary caregivers at home. While we would like to believe that starting school earlier will create smarter kids, the research does not support this notion. In fact, many believe that introducing formal instruction too early compromises a child's overall learning ability. Further, if the child doesn't respond to the premature exposure to formal instruction, there can be a diagnosis of A.D.D. In many of these cases however, I believe the child is suffering from an attachment disorder due to a lack of the essential experiences.

The child's earliest exposure to education must respect him as a whole person whose emotional growth is as important as his intellectual growth. Only in such a classroom will he have the best chance to learn about learning and to learn without the fear inducing elements that have been shown neurologically to inhibit retention.

Places of Wonder: Reggio Emilia

Be the bearers of joy, for without joy there is nothing.

— Loris Malaguzzi, founder

As part of my doctoral research, I compared educational environments that support the mental health as well as the intellectual growth of children. I was very impressed by both the philosophies of Rudolph Steiner (Waldorf Schools) and Maria Montessori, but I fell absolutely head-over-heels in love with Reggio Emilia. The Reggio Emilia Approach, as it is formally known, was developed by working parents in the Emilia region of northern Italy at the end of World War II. It embodies what I believe all children should experience as they enter the world beyond. Fulfilling the spirit of its founder, whom I quote above, Reggio Emilia educators see themselves as facilitators of joy and wonder, and have the goal to support individual paths to knowledge.

Reggio is built to keep a constant connection among children, parents and teachers. The child-centered approach to the curriculum requires that the teachers continually observe, listen, and document the child's classroom activity. Documentation in Reggio is a disciplined process that includes photographing ongoing student activity, which is then publicly displayed, and taking extensive written notes, which are shared with other teachers during their collaborative review sessions.

The documentation helps the teachers together determine "an emergent curriculum" which represents the children's greatest areas of interest. In one well described example, the Reggio teachers noticed that many of the children were coming to school with toy dinosaurs, which prompted a lot of spontaneous discussion and play. This unexpected interest led the teachers, in the spirit of emergent curriculum, to create a long-term project around dinosaurs. This project, which you can read about in *The Hundred Languages of Children, The Reggio Emilia Approach To Early Childhood Education,* took four months. The extended length of such a Reggio project allows for the subject matter to evolve and for some subjects to be examined repeatedly, leading to a more in-depth and joyous learning experience.

In the Reggio Approach, there is another educator: the environment; Reggio calls this the "third teacher." The physical classroom resembles more of a home than a traditional classroom through such accessories as curtained windows, comfy rugs and free-standing lamps. In addition, the students' work covers the walls not only in the hallway but in unexpected places like stairways and even bathrooms. The photographic murals, documenting the process behind the students' work, allows for children, parents and teachers to continually revisit and share the child's ongoing learning experience. This is different from conventional education, where the parent sees only the product of the classroom lesson plan. Seeing more of their child's learning process, parents can more fully understand and reflect the emotional experience of their child's school day.

Fulfilling Malaguzzi's belief in the one hundred languages of children, the Reggio school environment has at all times different areas provisioned for different learning styles. There is a mini-library for children naturally drawn to book learning, open space for dance and play acting, and of course the art studio, or *atelier.* The art studio is not just a place to learn to do art, it is a place to use art materials to learn.

These different environments allow children to share or "represent" their ideas in ways that suit them best. For example, in the library one can explore books and get more information about dinosaurs. In the atelier, under the guidance of the *atelierista,* the dedicated art teacher, children can learn more about dinosaurs through drawing, painting, and constructing a dinosaur in various ways. In the open space, students can transform themselves into dancing dinosaurs or create a stage for acting out their ideas about these prehistoric creatures.

At the center of the Reggio Approach are always the teachers. While they watch, listen, and record the children, they are learning how the children learn best. In the questions they ask, they are always seeking to better understand each child's thinking process. Learning at Reggio is not just about finding the right answers; it is directed at welcoming more questions and possibilities for exploration and debate. Most importantly the children are learning how to think in ways that will stay with them for the rest of their lives.

This brief discussion in no way does justice to the breadth and depth of this educational model. My purpose here is limited to describing an established framework in which the absolutely essential needs of idealizing, mirroring, twinship and adversarial can be met at school.

Great Expectations

As parents you have the right to ask for an educational environment that considers the absolutely essential needs of children so that your child will fully know herself, feel confident in her abilities, and have a desire to make a unique contribution in the world beyond. Teachers are your delegates to meet your children's needs in the classroom. Properly empowered, teachers can become mentors who do more than pour information into the child's brain. After all, "children are not just brains on a stick."

More books to read!

Miseducation: Pre-Schoolers at Risk, by David Elkind, Ph.D.

Your Child's Growing Mind: A Practical Guide To Brain Development and Learning From Birth Through Adolescence, by Jane Healy Ph.D.

How To Talk To Kids So Kids Can Learn: At Home and in School, by Adele Faber and Elaine Mazlish.

In Their Own Way: Discovering and Encouraging Your Child's Personal Learning Style, by Thomas Armstrong, Ph.D.

The Myth of the A.D.D. Child : 50 Ways to Improve Your Child's Behavior and Attention Span Without Drugs, Labels or Coercion, by Thomas Armstrong, Ph.D.

The One World Schoolhouse: Education Reimagined, by Salman Khan.

The Schools Our Children Deserve: Moving Beyond Traditional Classrooms and "Tougher Standards," by Alfie Kohn.

The Homework Myth: Why Our Kids Get Too Much Of A Bad Thing, by Alfie Kohn.

Part Six

Kitchen-Table Therapy

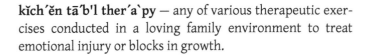

kĭch´ĕn tā´b'l ther´a`py — any of various therapeutic exercises conducted in a loving family environment to treat emotional injury or blocks in growth.

K itchen-table therapy is an opportunity for caregivers to enter empathically into a child's emotional world. Because of the premium placed on empathic involvement, it is an experience quite different from the daily routine, defined by schedules and the need for compliance. In the expression "kitchen-table therapy," I want parents to see how well suited they are to use the natural resources of family life to touch up gaps in development or to smoothe out ongoing conflicts. Wisdom, imagination, and playfulness are all that are required.

Act It Out, Play It Out, Work It Out

Play puts the child into an active position and converts felt deprivation into felt relief.

— A. J. Solnit

The adults in my practice use therapy to dig into the emotional pain arising from their life-struggles. The result of their hard work is always heightened self-awareness and an understanding about how and why they navigate their lives in the way that they do.

We all have parts of ourselves of which we are not fully aware. As a result, we naturally construct dramas using the people and events in our lives. This acting out, a human frailty, which if sufficiently reflected upon especially with a caring witness, can be the best way to uncover the truth in each of us.

In the behavior of children also, there is symbolism ever-present in their stories, which they use to send us messages about what they are experiencing and what parts of themselves they might be trying to bring to the surface. As parents we must observe and listen to these messages and respond in an attuned way, which is to say with as full an appreciation as possible of their entire experience. I ask you as a parent to never take your child's disruptive behavior, their acting out, at face value. He (or she) is not intending to be bad; he is using his everyday life experiences to express his innermost self.

Regress for Progress

In psychology, the term "regression" is commonly used to describe an attempt to return to an earlier stage of development where one employs behaviors that are considered inferior to one's present capability. It is usually a sign of mounting stress accompanied by a fear of moving forward in one's growth.

Regression can be adaptive or maladaptive. Adaptive (or healthy) regression is essential in adult life and in the life of a child. As adults we typically regress via recreational activities that provide pleasure not obtainable while meeting the demands of everyday life. We escape by listening to our favorite music, lose ourselves in a movie, commune with nature, or cheer wildly for our favorite sports team. In all of these restorative activities, we take a temporary break from our present reality.

Children typically use regression to revisit a developmental period that they have completed, where they feel masterful, in order to replenish themselves. As with adults, a child's attempt to regress indicates a need to escape from stress in their present life.

Behavior Is Just Behavior, How You Respond to the Behavior Defines It

At the outset all childhood regression is adaptive, or in "the service of the ego," to use Ernst Kris' expression. The caregiver's response strongly influences whether the child's regression continues to be adaptive or becomes maladaptive, which I define as regression that endangers the physical, emotional or intellectual health of the child. Kitchen-Table Therapy, including the methods described below, can keep a child's regression on an adaptive path and help to identify sources of stress. The following therapeutic activities are ones which I have found over the years to be most effective and readily adaptable to different family needs.

Filial Therapy

Drs. Louise and Bernard Guerney developed Filial Therapy, inspired by the belief that parents can be effective change agents in the lives of their children.

The technique leverages a child's natural and spontaneous fondness for play. The freedom with which children engage in play makes it an excellent tool to discover thoughts and feelings they seem otherwise hesitant to express. In this child-centered approach, parents set aside time to help children express their feelings in play activities. The Guerneys' method requires that parents master four skills, which they termed: structuring, empathic listening, child-centered imaginary play, and limit setting.

I have found that this approach is very effective in promoting new behaviors and attitudes in children, which are then transferred to daily family life. The beauty of this method is in its simplicity. There is not a lot to learn; it doesn't take very much time; and the rewards are bountiful. I have adapted the following explanation from *Filial Therapy: Strengthening Parent-Child Relationships* by Dr. Risë VanFleet. I highly recommend that you read this brief book and share it with another adult who will serve as your training partner. In it you will discover the importance of having someone give you supportive feedback as you attempt to master the technique.

The Power of Play

Many times conventional wisdom can prevent a parent from seeing playtime as an intimate parent-child interaction. Many of us have been taught that play is nothing more than an opportunity to keep a child busy. At best we purchase the latest age-appropriate "learning" toys, and as they get older we arrange play-dates for them to help them socialize. What we often do not realize is that play helps children both make sense out of their experiences and feel understood.

It can feel unnatural for parents to set aside time for Filial Therapy. Many of us have to work hard to find our playfulness again after years of being told to "grow-up" and act our age. For this reason, I ask you to find a friend or relative who can serve as your peer-training partner before you try this with your children. Peer-training and mock sessions will give you greater confidence when you start to conduct Filial Therapy with your son or daughter. You may want to consider using your training partner to conduct the initial therapy sessions with you as an observer if you unsure of your ability to meet the standards of Filial Therapy.

In the mock sessions you can play the adult or play the child and act out the absolutely essential experiences of happy, sad, angry and afraid within yourself. It can be an opportunity of self-discovery for the two of you to learn about yourselves and understand the complexities of communication. In turn, each of you can practice the difficult art of non-judgmental feedback. As a parent, we make judgments all day; but learning to be non-judgmental is critical to the success of play-therapy.

In play sessions with your child, watch out for these common problems:

- Feeling inhibited
- Wanting to tell your child how you feel about what they are playing out
- Feeling at a loss when having to describe what you think they are feeling
- Sticking to the structure and the limits

Keep these thoughts in mind as you read about the discrete elements of Filial Therapy below.

Step One: Structuring

Goal: Create a physical and emotional space for your child to be himself or herself in a structured environment.

Decide on a space in your home that can be temporarily dedicated to "special play times." To structure the space, you can use household objects such as easy-to-move furniture to create a clear entryway. Passage through the entryway will mark the start and end of a play session. This space need not be large; just enough to accommodate you and one child. It is my experience that most children love to play and are very pleased to know that a parent will join them.

Once the physical boundary is set, it will be important to talk about some other play rules. The following introductory speech, which you should feel free to adapt to your own speaking style, communicates what is important for the child to know.

> This is a special playtime for us. This is a space where you can say or do almost anything. If there is something you cannot do, I will tell you. We will play for about a half an hour. During this time you can have one bathroom break, so perhaps you would like to go the the bathroom before we start. There are some other rules for the playtime. If you break a rule I will let you know. If you break a rule more than once, we will end the playtime and try again another day.

It is important to tell your child five minutes before you have to end the play time; another reminder at one minute can be helpful to the transition out. Children often resist ending the play session at the limit you have set.

It is important to the structure to reflect and accept your child's feelings about wanting to continue with the play while staying firm on the time limit. Some parents will need to gently escort the child back through the entryway as a statement of finality. A statement like this helps ease the transition, "You really enjoyed our time together and you wish it didn't have to end. We will be sure to do it again soon."

Step Two: Empathic Listening

Goal: Allow your child to "act it out, play it out, and work it out" so that all feelings are expressed, heard and accepted without judgment.

This special playtime may be one of the few times that you as a parent can give yourself permission to just listen and accept what your child is saying. It can be a relief for both of you to have some conflict-free communication. In order for your child to feel free to express his true self you must practice "active listening," which requires you to reflect back to another person *in your own words* but without judgment what you are hearing them say.

It takes time to become comfortable and adept at active listening. At first you may be reflecting back what your child is feeling *in his words.* He or she may accuse you of parroting him. In such a moment, you can respond with, "I am just trying to understand"; and then try again with *new words.* For an excellent tutorial, read the classic book *How To Talk So Kids Will Listen, & Listen So Kids Will Talk,* by Adele Faber and Elaine Mazlish.

Step Three: Child-Centered Imaginary Play

Goal: Allow your child to create a theme in which he or she can be the director of the play.

The purpose of imaginary play is to give your child an opportunity to express the four human emotions: angry, sad, happy and afraid. Once freely expressed, these fundamental feelings become part of a richer and more complex way of communicating thoughts and ideas.

Certain toys can be excellent props and will inspire the themes that children wish to play out. Having such toys set aside in a tote bag or cardboard box works to make the time more special.

To help you get started, I list below some toys and the themes with which they are most commonly associated in play.

Family and Nurturance Themes
- Doll house
- Doll family and furniture

- Puppet families
- Baby bottles
- Kitchen set with pots, pans, and dishes
- Dress-up clothes

Themes of Aggression
- Small plastic figures like dinosaurs and warriors
- Foam aggression bats
- Bop (punching) bags and gloves

Themes of Fear and Injury
- Doctor's kit
- Police cars
- Ambulances
- Firetrucks

Themes of Expression and Mastery
- Toy phones
- Bop It toy
- Play-Doh or clay
- Blocks and construction toys
- Crayons and drawing paper

Once the toys are out, the child takes over. Your job is to reflect the experiences and feelings of the characters in the play. You should feel free to invite yourself in. If your child accepts the invitation be sure to ask him what role he wants you to take. It may take a couple of sessions for you and your child to be comfortable with this special play time and its reversal of roles; but you can expect that he will find the experience magical. For thirty minutes your child has the exquisite pleasure of telling you what to do! Without judgment!

Step Four: Limit Setting

Goal: To teach the child the consequences of his or her behavior and to give the parent practice at meaning what they say and following through.

The rules of this play therapy are designed to be easily managed by a young child. There are only a few; they are simple; and the introductory statement, "If there is something you cannot do I will let you know," makes a reasonable allowance for mistakes. But certain limits are essential for play; and limit setting is an important shared exercise between parent and child.

The simple rules are:

- No hurting oneself or the parent.
- No destruction of toys or contents of the play space
- Only one bathroom break per session

As I discussed in *The Mighty Milestones,* it is common for children to want to test their caregivers and may use playtime to do so. Such tests give parents the opportunity to show that they mean what they say without fear that they are harming their child by denying them their wish. The most the child will lose from not following the rules is the continuation of the play session; the parent can lessen this hurt by offering that, "We will try again on another day."

At this point, some readers may feel overwhelmed with all the requirements of Filial Therapy, especially if encountering it for the first time. Hopefully the example below will show how it all comes together.

Open Windows and Flying Babies: A Tragic Tale

Tyler was a toddler three with an attitude. His contrarian nature kept his parents constantly exhausted. The trouble started with the birth of his six-month-old brother. Tyler was at first upset by the arrival of his younger sibling, but now "he really loves him." When I asked what brought about the change in attitude, they looked at each other and smiled. "Bribery!" exclaimed the father.

To which the mother added, "And I just keep telling him how important it is to always love his brother and take care of him. It really works."

"Always loving his brother" was the only point of agreement between Tyler and his parents. He also loved all the toys that came his way whenever he behaved as a good brother should.

Tyler joined our next session, before which I explained that I would be conducting a child-centered play session that could be easily adapted at home.

In walked Tyler. I told him that in the playroom he could do and say almost anything and that I would let him know if something wasn't okay. He stomped over to the puppets that "were asleep" in a big basket in the corner and dumped them onto the floor to "wake them all up," declaring that "nap time is over." He then brought the dinosaur puppet over to the infant doll in the highchair, who got a loud growl from this prehistoric creature.

The parents honored their commitment as silent observers.

Looking around for other characters, he brought the black cat puppet into the play. After a brief battle with the dinosaur, the black cat lay defeated on the floor; and the dinosaur flew back into the basket.

"Dinosaur growled at the baby," I said tracking the events.

"Yes," responded Tyler with a grin.

"Dinosaur had a fight with the cat."

"Yes."

"Cat is lying on the floor."

"Yes," said Tyler continuing our dialogue.

"Dinosaur is back in the basket."

"Yes, he is sleeping," said the little director.

His parents sat quietly and saw that my simple observations were all that it took for him to see me as a potential play partner. I did nothing more than narrate his experiences without judging his actions.

Tyler scanned the room deep in thought. Spotting my Fisher-Price dollhouse on a high shelf he asked me to take it down. He emptied the contents onto the floor; and sitting cross-legged he began to arrange the family, the furniture, the car, and the dog.

"Can I play?" I asked sitting down next to him.

He nodded with a charming toddler grin.

"Okay, what do you want me to do?"

He cut me off with a curt, "No."

"Okay, you tell me if you want me to do something."

He quietly filled the dollhouse rooms with furniture. When he got to the nursery, he tried to to fit two babies into the cradle without success.

"You take this," he said handing me a baby.

"What do you want me to do with the baby?"

He said nothing. Instead, he grabbed the other baby and shoved it out of the nursery window.

"The baby flying," he laughed.

My eyes on Tyler, I heard his mother shift in her chair. To her credit, she kept quiet.

"You do it too," he commanded me.

"You want me to make this baby go out the window?"

"Yes, I don't want them in there!"

"Okay, out goes the baby," I said while pushing it out the nursery window. "What should I do now?"

"Make babies stay out. Out of house," said Tyler, a man of few words.

In my follow-up, I asked Tyler's parents for their reactions. His acting out in the playroom had upset them both, and they wondered why I didn't tell him that babies should never be pushed out of a window or that the dinosaur may have scared the baby.

I explained that his behavior in play was just a metaphor, an opportunity to express and work out his conflicted feelings about his brother, feelings for which he was not rewarded in everyday life.

In response to their anxiety that Tyler might confuse the world of play with the world of everyday, I explained that the structuring of this special play in both time and space enables the parent to communicate that the play is different from life. And the limit setting of play therapy helps parents and children practice important rules, such as those that prevent actual harm to family members.

Playing in the Sand Tray

The therapeutic use of sand in a tray extends back to the 1920s, when British pediatrician/psychiatrist Margaret Lowenfeld first introduced "The World Technique," also described as "World Play."

Dr. Lowenfeld believed that children feel most comfortable expressing their innermost thoughts while playing with small toys or miniatures and that children are naturally drawn to sand and water play. Combining these two experiences, she was the first to use open boxes — one filled with sand, the other with water — to encourage children to build their wet or dry "world" in the sand. Also offered were boxes of small objects that could be used to create a story, an expression that would inevitably describe the child's inner state of being.

Doing Nothing Is Doing Something

The World Technique required no analysis. She found that allowing children to build their own worlds in the sand put them in charge and that this in turn encouraged them to "express the inexpressible." In the tradition of humanistic psychology, the World Technique assumes that children are capable of working through their problems once they can express themselves without the fear of being judged.

Another important contributor to this method was Dora Kalff, a Jungian analyst who studied with Lowenfeld and coined the term "sandplay." She believed that children used sand to play out experiences of healthy individuation and self-sufficiency as well as to express conflicts. She also found that openly displaying the miniature (theme) toys on shelves encouraged children to pick objects that would create a communication link between their conscious and unconscious minds.

Both Lowenfeld and Kalff used the sandtray to create an opportunity for the child to discover parts of the self that may have gone "underground." Because this technique avoids judging what the "sandplayer" is doing, it provides the child with the experience of having an adventure within the security of the tray. They limited the role of the therapist to witnessing and empathically reflecting what the child is expressing in the developing story. Their interpretation of the therapist's role, novel at the time, has become a core concept in the conduct of all child-centered play therapy.

Play with a Purpose: Secure Independence

My use of the sandtray with children has inspired this Kitchen-Table adaptation. (To ease the housekeeping, I use uncooked white rice instead of sand.) In all my years of practice, I have not once encountered a child that wasn't drawn to my trays. They (see the photograph below) are part of a rolling set of drawers that I keep in my sandtray alcove.

Each drawer is lined with a plastic tray and is removable. As you can see, I keep my collection of miniatures on shelves alongside the cart. Different categories of objects are housed in different cubbies. My collection of miniatures covers the same themes used in Filial work: family figures, animals, furniture, and buildings. My rice tray world has a full fleet of vehicles, including transportation for mere earthlings as well as time and space travelers.

In setting up your own sand (rice) center at home, you should start with the following:

- Two large, covered plastic containers. The kind used for under-bed storage works best. The dimensions are good, and the attached wheels provide for easy transportation. If the container has a blue cover, you can place it underneath to represent water. Otherwise you can line the bottom of the container with blue contact paper.

- Rice or sand-box sand
- Cups for water (if using sand)
- Paper towels!
- Small plastic tarp for under the tray play area
- Small bookcase with open shelves, or several shoe boxes
- Assortment of miniature toys and figurines organized by theme. Collecting the miniatures is less time consuming and expensive then you might think. Sources include discount stores, pieces of old toys and games, yard sales and flea markets. And if all else fails, search the internet for: sand tray toys.
- Play-Doh, construction paper, pipe cleaners (for making objects)

The example below demonstrates what can happen in the tray.

Fenced-In Feelings

Aimee was just turning seven when I met her. In my initial consultation, her mother had described her as "a good girl" with major sleep issues. During the day she willingly assisted her mother with the family chores but was happiest when she was left alone to work on her beaded jewelry and friendship bracelets.

It was decided that she would accompany her mother for the next session so that we could talk about some of her fears.

Upon entering my playroom, Aimee was immediately drawn to the rice tray alcove. For ten minutes she slid the rice through her fingers back and forth. From time to time, she filled my small plastic cups with rice only to empty them back into the tray. She repeated these actions over and over as her mother and I sat quietly and watched. Looking up at her mother she smiled.

"You are enjoying yourself," I said.

"Yes, what are those for?" she replied still smiling, eyeing the miniatures on the shelves.

"They are objects that you can put in the tray, any way that you like. Sometimes kids like to build a world using these toys."

"Can I?" she asked her mom.

"Yes, of course," her mom replied confidently; but I sensed apprehension.

Aimee reached up and grabbed the father and mother figurines from the "family shelf."

Looking over my collection, she discovered a small box of artificial plants and trees. Holding the father and mother in one hand, she started her rice tray world by planting a robust tree in one corner. She then firmly placed the mother alongside the tree, digging her in as you would an umbrella in the sand on a windy day.

Next, the two-story miniature home reached its destination in the opposite corner of the tray. Aimee carefully scanned the shelves for her next pick. She seemed to focus on a miniature antique cash register but then placed the father figure on his knees in front of the home. Both hands free, she took down the cash register and studied it from every angle, trying to understand what it was for. She placed it in front of the father and stretched out his bendable arms. Out of the corner of my eye I noticed a subtle change in the expression on the face of Aimee's mother.

Sorting through my "environments box," Aimee found a wood and wire fence. Placing it it in the tray, she discovered a gap in the fence where the slats were missing. Next, with careful deliberation she chose some animals. The first three looked ferocious, but then she chose a friendly looking, small, white dog.

"She is so cute," she giggled as she placed it with the others behind the fence.

Aimee stood back to take in what she had assembled. For a few more minutes she used the toy shovel to pat down all the rice in the tray. After smoothing it out, she carefully picked up the dog, using the gap in the fence to get it to the other side.

"The cute dog is outside the fence," I said.

"Yes," was her only reply. Her face remained still as her fingers continued to smoothe the rice.

As our time was coming to a close, I gave her a two minute warning and asked if there was anything else she wanted to do to her world.

"No," she smiled. "I'm done."

Looking at her mom, she asked, "Should we put everything back?" I let them both know that it was fine to leave it all in place. Aimee's face brightened when I asked for permission to photograph it.

"Yes, could we?" she asked her mom.

Mom nodded her permission. I photographed her creation and showed them the digital result. Smiling, Aimee then asked her mother to take a picture with her phone camera. Mom complied, and now all three of us had a visual record of the rice tray session.

Often the hands know how to solve a riddle with which the intellect has wrestled in vain.

— Carl Jung

In the follow-up session, Aimee's mom confessed her awe at the effectiveness of the single sandtray experience. Her daughter had loved it; she so much wanted to do it again that Mom agreed to set up a rice tray at home.

Mom was impressed with how quickly Aimee set up a representational world in the rice tray which revealed family dynamics that we had not yet addressed. Tension had been rising between husband and wife over the amount time he was working both at home and away. When Aimee asked her father why he was never around, his standard reply was, "I have to work so that I can buy nice things for this family."

Her face tense, Mom added, "I am so very tired of hearing him say that. I think it is just an excuse. He really doesn't like spending time with us, and it makes us both angry. I don't say anything about this anymore. Nothing ever works."

We came to understand that Aimee was working hard both to make sense out of and to do something about the anger in the household. In the rice tray, she could safely dramatize this anger to caring witnesses as well as express her own aggressive feelings about the tension in her real-life home. Once Aimee's parents understood that her fear of her *own* aggression could be keeping her awake at night, they made the sacrifices that parents do to restore happiness to their child's world.

Touch-Up Work

No one completes human development in the first pass, which is childhood. Like a newly painted room that when it is dry has some patches of the old color peaking through, one need not repaint the whole room; we only need to touch up certain areas to create a more finished appreciation of the new color.

The exercises below have been a tremendous help to the families in my practice. Spending time with your children in these ways will encourage deeper feelings of attachment and enhance their ability to focus and pay attention. Each is designed to meet essential needs that are not always adequately addressed during normal daily routines. They are just a few examples of the creative ways you can both help your children and discover personal areas that may need touching up.

As with other *Kitchen-Table Therapy* activities, the success of the exercises below begin and end with empathy, an art that requires selfless patience on the part of the parent but one which produces enduring, almost magical results.

Be My Baby

Goal: Allow the child to use fantasy to go back to an earlier time of life. Children naturally want to re-experience the security of less challenging times. Giving them this privileged and private time with you will cut down on their need to act it out.

Parent Benefit: Reduce "babyish" behavior in your child, eliminating the need to say, "Stop acting like a baby." While setting aside time to allow the child to re-experience early development, you can enjoy those wonderful moments, knowing that you are shoring him up for his daily life. These experiences can also help to alleviate intense feelings of sibling rivalry when a new child enters the family.

Techniques: Use photos or videos to "go back in time." Using the phrase, "When you were a baby ... we used to..." is sure to grab their attention. Sometimes parents will say, "I really miss playing some games we played then ..." The classics *Peek-a-Boo, Itsy Bitsy Spider,* and *This Little Piggy* never seem to fail. Baby lotion for massages, blankets, and baby toys help the exercise.

Guidelines: During the initial rounds of this exercise, some children may need more time to trust that they can return to babyishness without judgment. It is important to set aside private time for this touch-up work to eliminate some of the awkwardness that can occur. You are giving your child permission to "be a baby" for a limited time so you can both remember and reinforce your early attachment to one another. Most parents find that playing just before bedtime works best for baby-games.

Parent Favorite: *This Little Piggy* toe massage.

I Only Have Eyes for You

Goal: Reinforcing attachment.

Parent Benefit: A playful way to connect with your child.

Technique: Parent and child gaze into each others' eyes as long as possible. Each takes a turn at it, competing to see who can do it longer without turning away or breaking into laughter.

Guidelines: Making eye-contact, while an important social skill, is not easy for everyone. This exercise may take some time before it feels comfortable. It should be pleasurable for both parent and child.

Parent Favorite: Gazing into their child's eyes while singing a full verse from "I Only Have Eyes For You."

Four Little Boxes

Goal: Help children identify and express the four basic emotions of happy, sad, angry and afraid. Having one's feelings acknowledged by a caregiver gives a sense of connectedness, which is essential for a child to build their own empathic ability.

Parent Benefit: The child will manage her daily feelings better by talking them out rather than acting them out.

Techniques: Explain to your child that both adults and children have feelings about everything all day long. Invite the child to imagine one, two, three, four "little covered boxes inside your head." Each box is full of one feeling. One has happy feelings; one has sad feelings; one has mad feelings; and one has scary feelings. Drawing and labeling these imaginary boxes on paper helps illustrate the concept. A good starter exercise, which children usually enjoy, is to ask your child to draw these boxes herself with a face inside each one which represents one of the four basic emotions. You can ask your child, "What color is the box? How big? Is the cover hard to lift off or easy?" Parents find this metaphor useful to encourage the exploration and expression of feelings.

Guidelines: It is important to know that children bump into experiences each day that will require them to use and make sense of the four human emotions. They open each box every-day in an attempt to communicate what they are learning about themselves. When we accept their feelings with under-standing, we can elicit their natural cooperation more easily.

Parent Favorite: Use four shoeboxes to transfer visualizations and drawings to three-dimensional objects. After labeling the boxes, the parent and child come together to make a list of feeling words in each category — happy, sad, angry and afraid. Write the words on index cards that are stored in their appropriate box. Older children love owning their feelings in this way. When a child feels especially frustrated, the parent can encourage her to use the cards in the boxes to help talk out her feelings.

Read My Face

Goal: Developing empathy in children.

Parent Benefit: Teach social skills and interpersonal focus.

Techniques: Sit with your child while flipping through magazines, looking at picture books, or watching television. Point out facial expressions and ask the child which feeling he thinks the person or animal is expressing.

Guidelines: Children usually love playing this game with a caregiver. Since the goal is to teach empathy, it is important for the caregiver to empathize with the child during the game: let him have his own opinion about what the character is feeling. To extend the play you can ask the child why he thinks the person or animal is feeling the way that they do. Most children are happy to create more elaborate stories if they know that they will be free from judgment for doing so.

Parent Favorite: You can paste the magazine photos and illustrations into a book of faces, which can be added to the bedtime reading collection. Scrapbooks, construction paper, photo albums — all available at craft and stationary stores — can be used to create this personal book. You can add photographs of friends and relatives to make this book more intimate.

Venn Diagrams: Mixed Feelings

Goal: Help children make sense out of ambivalence.

Parent Benefit: A simple way to explain contradictory feelings.

Technique: Draw large circles on two pieces of translucent paper such as wax or tracing paper. In one circle write some words describing what your child is feeling. For example, "I hate my brother." In the other circle write their opposite sentiment. For example, "I like playing outside with my brother." Take the two circles and overlap them. Point to the overlapping space and explain that a person can have two opposite feelings at the same time. This is ambivalence!

Guidelines: Be sure to fill each circle with opposing feelings that are true for your child. Children will not respond favorably to this exercise if you use it to tell them what they *should* be feeling.

Parent Favorite: Once your child understands this concept you can create a venn diagram with your hands by circles made with your thumb and index finger. This silent signal of ambivalence can be useful for quick communication inside the family.

Just Plain Old Puppets

Goal: Have child play out a scene with puppets that parallels a conflict in his real life.

Parent Benefit: Your child can safely act out feelings that he seems unable to express.

Techniques: Brown paper lunch bags are the basic start for plain old puppets. You can keep it simple with a box of crayons or markers or visit a craft store to purchase items that can be used to make more elaborate puppets.

To help the child act out hard-to-express feelings, it is important for him to create puppets that will help him get close to those feelings. The following prompts from the caregiver can get the characters onto paper:

"Let's make a puppet that is you."

"Let's make a puppet that is you when (describe an event that seems to elicit great happiness, anger, sadness or fear)." Examples: "Let's make a puppet that is you when Mommy or Daddy is angry with you/ your sister takes a toy away from you/ you are playing catch with Dad."

Next, in order to create the puppet play, ask your child to create puppets that represent the other person with whom you think the child might be in conflict. For example, "Let's make a puppet that is your brother when he pushes you off the swing."

If the child seems unable to get started, the parent can create a puppet of their own which reflects one of the four basic emotions. It is important for him to create several puppets so that he has an array of characters to use during the drama. During the play, he will be actively engaged in two-fisted puppetry (no pun intended) with many puppet-changes in order to express the right emotion.

You can construct a small portable theatre by placing a curtain rod between two chairs. A pair of colorful inexpensive curtains can be closed and opened during showtime.

Guidelines: Puppetry is another opportunity for children to express deep feelings through fantasy.

While identifying with the puppet character, the child stays at a safe distance from the situation they are playing out. This allows the child to use the experience to more objectively create new endings/solutions. Your job is to be an empathic witness.

Parent Favorite: Once established, you can use puppetry more informally during the day to get at unexpressed feelings. Puppet-play can be especially useful to understand the distorted expression of adversarial needs by your child. You can have him act out an adversarial exchange or puppet debate that ends with "agreeing to disagree."

Author's note: Therapeutic puppetry is rich with opportunity. Thanks to the internet, you have many resources at your fingertips including starter kits and guidebooks.

Living Happily Ever After: Tell Me a Story

Goal: Use storytelling to help children with fear and anxiety.

Parent Benefit: This is an activity that will provide your child with the essential experience of idealizing.

Techniques: Create a plot for a story based on a current issue with which your child is struggling, for example, a fear of sleeping in the dark. Have the main character resolve the problem in a positive way. An option is to let your child tell a story to which you respond with a story of your own using the same plot and characters but with a more positive ending.

Guidelines: Be sure not to use these stories to deny the character's feelings. The story is an opportunity for the child to see a problem from a distance and have someone successfully solve a seemingly impossible issue. Treat the character with the same respect as you would your child while creating a new ending. Children are comforted by the wisdom of these stories.

Parent Favorite: Extend this technique by telling your child that you read about someone with a problem just like his in a non-fiction book or magazine about kids. With obvious relief, you can share the resolution, letting the child in on the great discovery you made. Don't be surprised if months down the road your son asks, "Mom, you know that book about me that you found, can you read it again?"

Look at Me Playing

Goal: Use games of mastery to witness and respond to your child's developing skills.

Parent Benefit: These experiences are filled with opportunities to meet the essential need of mirroring.

Techniques: Set aside time to sit with or watch your child engaging in any activity (including video games) that demonstrate skill or innate talent. Watch for ways that your child is taking risks, persevering, making decisions, and handling challenges. Be aware of emerging feelings of excitement as well as frustration and disappointment.

Guidelines: Use yourself as a witness and narrator. What is important here is how your child feels about what she is doing, *not* how you feel about it. As your child plays, she is making sense of the four human emotions as well as shoring up her confidence. Your role is to point out what you believe she is feeling during the activity as well as pointing out areas of improved skill.

Parent favorite: Electronic audio game *Bop It* by Hasbro is a toy for children and parents alike.

Reacting quickly to the commands Bop It, Pull, and Twist develops hand-eye coordination as well as focusing attention. The game is frustratingly fun and is hard to put down. It can be played solo or shared with a partner. Try *Bop It Extreme* if you dare!

Dinnertime: Food for Thought

Goal: Use this time to reinforce essential experiences and relationships. Help children to develop social skills while practicing patience, non-competitive assertiveness, and thinking well of others.

Parent Benefit: Consistent use of this time in this way will promote family harmony and provide mirroring experiences for each child. The creation of an empathic circle around the dinner table can become a trusted idealizing ritual for all your children and hopefully one that they will carry into the next generation.

Techniques: To help children feel a sense of purpose, assign age appropriate tasks so each member of the family can make a dinner-table contribution. Reinforce healthy boundaries and limit setting by making sure everyone is present at the designated time. Dinner begins with a "go-around" that consists of each person telling the family one good thing that happened during the day. Sometimes this can be difficult, especially for someone who has had an experience that is worrisome or upsetting. (They can ask for a pass during the go-around.) Depending on the size of your family, each person is allowed to speak for about three minutes. (Where limit setting is difficult, a loud egg timer is useful.) Another rule is that there is no interrupting, judgment or criticism allowed when a family member speaks. Dinner closes with Mom or Dad reflecting back (mirroring) each person's exciting accomplishment for the day. In mirroring, it is important to speak about the feeling associated with the experience, not just the facts.

Guidelines: Consider the family dinner sacred. Understandably, not all families can do this every evening; but even a few every week can make a huge difference. It is a time to set aside everything for the sake of helping your child develop a cohesive self. This happens best inside the structure of a family that listens, encourages, and thinks well of you and your accomplishments. Children who are unaccustomed to speaking well of themselves may be reluctant to share their feelings of achievement until you model it a few times. Continued unwillingness to share daily successes will alert you to the need to engage some of the exercises above.

Parent Favorite: Change the go-around exercise by asking each member of the family to say one nice thing about each person at the table. Remember, it is difficult not to like someone who you *know* likes you!

Epilogue:
What Comes Next

If there is light in the soul,
  there will be beauty in the person.
If there is beauty in the person,
  there will be harmony in the house.
If there is harmony in the house,
  there will be order in the nation.
If there is order in the nation,
  there will be peace in the world.

— Chinese proverb

It all begins with empathy. Empathy is neither forgiveness nor unbounded acceptance of all behavior. It is the reflection of another's emotional experience so that they feel understood — understood well enough to feel that they are a part of the world in which they live so that alienation does not become a slowly spreading cancer in their soul.

In this book I have emphasized that in all stages of your child's development the greatest growth will result from the responses of an empathic environment, and that from these steady and predictable experiences of being understood will come the development of your child's own empathic skills.

Fluency in the language of empathy will be a distinguishing factor in your child's adult success, both personally and professionally. In our time, empathy has become not just a parenting skill or a family skill, it is a world skill. Advances in travel and communication have made the world a smaller place; there is now greater interdependence among the previously less inter-dependent, separate cultures around the globe. Your children will need to understand the perspectives of others, enabling them to meet the enormous need for conflict resolution in a world where we are more frequently being bombarded with foreign beliefs and ideas. But hardwired into all people of all nations are the feelings of happy, sad, angry and afraid. Showing another that you understand their emotional experience is a way to create a bond with someone who may be very different from you.

The influence gained with another person who anticipates that their feelings will be understood cannot be overstated. People either talk out or act out their feelings. As I finish writing this book, the all-too-frequent mass shootings in the U.S. show us that there is far too much acting out, with devastating consequences to the families of both the victims and those ill individuals who did not get the proper treatment in time. And after each incident, we collectively wonder how a human being could possibly commit such a horrible act. People act out violently, I believe, because they do not trust that there is someone who will listen.

In his book *The Science of Evil: On Empathy and the Origins of Human Cruelty*, neuroscientist Simon Baron-Cohen, Ph.D., describes two important components of empathy. The first is the cognitive ability to accurately identify the feelings of another, and the second is possessing enough emotional sensitivity to appropriately respond to them. Like many others, he believes that the experience of emotional neglect in childhood contributes to "an erosion of empathy," a phrase he has coined to displace the idea that evil is the cause of cruelty. If it is our species, rather than a divine power, who creates cruelty, then we are all in a position to change the world, one child at a time. As we, both as citizens of the U.S. and of the world, search for a lasting solution to everyday violence, I consider reversing the erosion of empathy to be an elegant and powerful way to begin.

So, dear reader, to address the far-reaching problems caused by empathy erosion, I would like you to consider how you can use what you have learned from this book. You now possess an informed understanding of how healthy human development creates the capacity for genuine understanding as well as an awareness of what can destroy it. And since emotional development is never perfectly completed in early childhood, we are compelled to observe and reflect upon our own adult acting out, with caring witnesses, in order to keep ourselves on the unending path of human growth.

My greatest hope for this book is that it will serve as a catalyst to minimize human cruelty through the everyday practice of mutual understanding.

Let us begin.

Endnote

And the day came when the risk it took to remain tight inside the bud was more painful than the risk it took to blossom.

— Anais Nin

Ten years ago I met a man who has supported and guided the wisdom of this book.

A friend in common encouraged our first meeting, on a warm July afternoon, quite sure that we would be "a good match." And we were a good match indeed, extraordinary thinking-partners right from the start. We began with lunch at Cafe Mozart on the Upper West Side of Manhattan. Two hours of talking wasn't enough, so we continued our conversation while ambling through Central Park.

He fascinated me, this man whose interests included psychoanalysis, the stock market, poetry, astrology, dramatic writing , music and politics. Another three hours flew by; while resting in Shakespeare's Garden, we decided to go for dinner.

Ten years later we still smile when recollecting our seven-and-a-half- hour first date, which ended when he hailed me a cab that would take me to Penn Station so I could train it back to Long Island.

"Call me when you arrive home safely," he hugged me goodbye.

Looking up at him, I slowly shook my head and wondered aloud, "Where did you come from?"

"I sprang from your unconscious," he replied without hesitation. "And that book you told me that you would love to write, Parent Fatigue Syndrome? It's going to sell like hotcakes!"

Two years and many conversations later we would become husband and wife, the start of an ongoing collaboration that has inspired many things, including this book.

In Blethyn Hulton I have found a superb editor/collaborator who steals my commas when I am not looking and steers me away from those darn dangling participles. He also has an uncanny ability to synthesize information and capture my thoughts at the same time, making the writing of this book a most wonderfully creative and energizing experience. For all of this, I am grateful.

Most importantly I am indebted to the *Blethyn Factor*, the rare experience of being supported unconditionally by a highly attuned, non-competitive individual whose goal (and talent) is to help others discover, liberate, and use their innate abilities so that they can be their best.

Hopefully this book will help others do the same for themselves and their children.

Index